The *Catholic* Way to Pray

AN ESSENTIAL GUIDE FOR ADULTS

The Catholic way to pray

AN ESSENTIAL GUIDE FOR ADULTS

Kathleen Glavich, SND

TWENTY THIRD *23rd*
PUBLICATIONS
www.23rdpublications.com

TWENTY-THIRD PUBLICATIONS
A Division of Bayard
One Montauk Avenue, Suite 200
New London, CT 06320
(860) 437-3012 or (800) 321-0411
www.23rdpublications.com

Cover image: ©iStockphoto.com/creativeeye99

The Scripture passages contained herein are from the *New Revised
Standard Version of the Bible*, copyright ©1989, by the Division of
Christian Education of the National Council of Churches in the
U.S.A. All rights reserved.

ISBN 978-1-58595-755-2
Library of Congress Catalog Card Number: 2009926116
Printed in the U.S.A.

Contents

Introduction

Like all good Jews, the apostles prayed the daily Jewish prayers. They prayed in their synagogues and in the Temple in Jerusalem. But after meeting Jesus, the apostles were drawn to deepen their prayer. Here was a holy man who enjoyed intimate union with God and who even spent whole nights rapt in prayer. No wonder the apostles begged Jesus, "Teach us how to pray."

Chances are, you too have been praying for some time, perhaps even daily. Now in your journey of faith you are seeking to increase your understanding of prayer. And you are ready to broaden your repertoire of prayer styles, in particular, to move more deeply into Catholic ways to pray, a tradition that has a long, rich history.

In this book you will find the information and inspiration to jumpstart your prayer life as a Catholic. May it be only the beginning of an exciting adventure for you as you walk more closely in the footsteps of Jesus Christ, who leads us to the Father through the Holy Spirit.

A note on language: As a pure spirit, God has no gender, and both masculine and feminine images for God can enrich prayer. However, it's been a long-standing tradition to use masculine pronouns for God, and they occur in our liturgy and prayers. So far, attempts to address this discrepancy in our language have been awkward and unsatisfactory. In this book, then, you will find masculine pronouns for God.

1

Prayer:
Connecting to God

We came from God's hands, and our destiny is to live with our Triune God forever. While on earth, we yearn for God, as St. Augustine expressed in his famous prayer: "Our hearts are restless, O God, until they rest in you." Philosopher Blaise Pascal described this ache as having a hole in our hearts that can only be filled by God. Incredibly, God also longs to be with us. C.S. Lewis commented, "People seeking God is like a mouse seeking a cat." God, the almighty maker of the universe, loves us with a powerful, unconditional love. His love is so tremendous that in order for us to be with him eternally, he stooped to become a human being like us. Then, as the God-man Jesus Christ, God actually underwent death. His resurrection confirmed his promise that we too would rise someday.

In this life we can come in contact with this good God through prayer, traditionally defined as "the lifting of the mind and heart to God." Whenever we think of or speak with God, we are praying. It is said that most people pray more and better than they think they do.

St. Teresa of Avila defined prayer as "a conversation with one whom you know loves you." It involves both speaking *and* listening. Just as communication is key in the development of a human love relationship, prayer is essential if we wish to intensify our relationship with God. Prayer is as necessary for our spiritual life as breathing is for our physical life. God doesn't need our prayer, but we do!

Here are some other good reasons to pray:

- Knowing that God exists makes sense out of the universe. Praying to God gives meaning to our lives.

- Prayer makes us better persons. Through prayer we receive graces to live the Gospel values and grow in virtues like faith, hope, and charity.

- Prayer removes temporal punishment due for sins, that is, the punishment that helps make up for our forgiven sins either on earth or in purgatory.

- Prayer is life's most intoxicating high, the peak experience.

- In prayer we find satisfaction, fulfillment, and peace.

- God desires that we pray.

Growth in Prayer

The progression of prayer can be compared to the stages of communication between people involved in a love relationship. At first the two talk a lot: face-to-face, on the phone, by e-mail, or text messaging. They wish to learn as much as possible about each other and in turn to reveal information, even secrets, about themselves. As the relationship deepens, talking is not that necessary. The couple can read each other's minds and communicate just by a glance. Over time, two people in love are content simply to be in each other's presence wordlessly. Similarly, we begin speaking to God and eventually may enjoy contemplation (wordless prayer) and union with God. In the words of the thirteenth-century mystic Juliana of Norwich, "Prayer one-eth the soul to God."

Fortunately, communication with God can be instant. First of all, God is everywhere and on call 24/7. God knows our very thoughts and sees our every action. As St. Paul preached, "In him we live and move and have our being" (Acts 17:28). In addition, we enjoy the mystery of the divine indwelling: God dwells within our very being. God tugs at our hearts for attention. At any time we can sink down into the cave of our hearts for an encounter with God.

HOW GOD SPEAKS

God holds up his side of the conversation in several ways:

- All of God's creation—stars, mountains, trees, lakes, snow, flowers, dogs, our own marvelous bodies—shouts out God's love for us and declares God's power and glory. Rightly Simone Weil said, "The world is God's language to us."

- God speaks to us in Sacred Scripture, revealing himself as our lover and savior.

- God speaks to us through other people. Their words or actions can convey a divine message.

- God says things to us through our experiences, even our dreams.

- Most intimately, God speaks to us through our thoughts, either a progression of ideas or a sudden realization.

As you advance in the spiritual life, your prayer preferences will change. You may be content to pray formula prayers or to speak to God simply and spontaneously, and then suddenly you find that you relish reflecting on Scripture instead, or even just sitting in silence, aware of God's presence. The basic rule for prayer is *pray as you can, not as you can't*. In the end, prayer is a gift from God!

2

Five Forms
of Prayer

The *Catechism of the Catholic Church* defines the following five basic forms of prayer. These forms, or themes, differentiate prayers, but some prayers are a combination of two or more forms.

1. Blessing/Adoration

God blesses us, that is, gives us good gifts. In return we bless, or adore, God, which means we acknowledge and celebrate God's greatness. Adoration is the primary stance of human beings before God, who is our creator, our savior, and the master of the universe. God is the unnameable one, the utterly Other, a profound mystery whom we will never understand and on whom we are totally dependent. Who can gaze at the ocean, a sunset, or a newborn baby and not respond with awe and   ɔ worship is a natural respor
ment obliges us to worship.
Catholics adore God al01

is called *latria*. We do not adore the Blessed Virgin Mary and the other saints who, though holy, are still merely human beings. The honor or veneration we give to the saints is called *dulia*; the honor we give to Mary, the Mother of God, is called *hyperdulia*.

BLESSINGS

A **blessing** is a sacramental that asks God's favor and grace upon a person or object. (A **sacramental** is a sacred sign through which grace is given by the merits of Jesus and the saints through prayers of the Church.) A blessing is usually imparted by an ordained minister but can also be given by a lay person. The words of a blessing may be accompanied by out-stretched hands, the laying on of hands, the Sign of the Cross, or the sprinkling of holy water.

2. Petition

Someone quipped, "As long as there are tests, there will be prayers in public schools." We depend on God for everything, not just for help in tests. Jesus advised us to ask the Father in his name for what we need. The main thing we stand in need of is forgiveness. Therefore, we express our contrition and we petition the Father to forgive us. We also ask God that his kingdom of peace and justice come. We can request God to give us anything else for ourselves, even trivial things, confident that he will hear us. A prayer of petition is an act of faith.

3. Intercession

All members of the Church are interdependent. When others are in need, we turn trustingly to our good God with prayers of supplication for them. In this way we imitate Jesus, who is constantly interceding for us. Scripture assures us that we can help one another by our prayers:

> I urge that supplications, prayers, intercessions, and thanksgivings be made for everyone, for kings and all who are in high positions, so that we may lead a quiet and peaceable life in all godliness and dignity. This is good, and pleases God our Savior.
> (1 Timothy 2:1–3)

Catholics pray for the deceased. We believe that if they are in purgatory, our prayers will hasten their purification process. We have the custom of sending the grieving family a Mass card informing them that we have had a Mass said for the repose of the soul of their loved one. We can have this Mass offered at a parish or contact a religious congregation that for a donation will have a Mass said and provide a Mass card.

A *spiritual bouquet* is a gift of prayers and good deeds offered for the recipient and his or her intentions. We list our promises in a card, for example, "I offer three Hail Marys, three Our Fathers, and three acts of charity." These gifts can be creative, such as "five extra minutes of prayer each day for a week" or "working two days in a soup kitchen."

4. Thanksgiving

When we receive gifts, graces, and favors, it's only common courtesy to express our gratitude to God with prayers of thanksgiving. Jesus shows that he values this form of prayer when he expresses disappointment that out of ten cured lepers only one is thoughtful enough to thank him. Meister Eckhart, a mystic of the Middle Ages, commented, "If the only prayer you say in your entire life is thank you, it will be enough."

5. Praise

When someone exhibits an admirable quality or achieves something, our response is to acknowledge this with a compliment. Likewise, moved by God's power, goodness, or love, we praise him. Glorifying God because he is God is the chief occupation of the angels and saints in heaven. Incidentally, the word *alleluia* means "praise God." (*Hallel* is Hebrew for praise and *yah* is the first syllable of Yahweh, God's personal name.) And *amen*, the word we use to conclude prayers, means "I agree."

Love

Sometimes we are so taken with God and God's love and mercy that we pray prayers of sheer love. Edward Farrell's wrote a book entitled *Prayer Is a Hunger*. This title is a good description of prayer. It is a longing to be with God, the object of our love. In a real love relationship, neither person is concerned about getting something out of it. Each one desires not to receive, but to give. The same is true for our relationship with God. We spend time with God because we know it pleases him. And in prayer we let God love us.

3

Varieties
of Prayers

Prayer comes in as many different styles as there are ways to cook potatoes. You have probably experienced most of the following kinds of prayer.

- Vocal (said aloud) prayer or mental (thought) prayer
- Personal (private) prayer or group (communal) prayer
- Traditional formulas, such as the Our Father and Hail Mary
- Prayers composed by saints and other people. Sometimes these express the exact thoughts and feelings we have in our hearts.
- Our original written compositions
- Spontaneous (informal) prayer
- Singing or listening to a hymn
- *Meditation*, that is, thinking about God or the things of God. We can meditate on Scripture passages, prayer books, pictures, or our own experiences.

- Affective prayer, which is responding to God with various sentiments, such as love and adoration

- *Contemplation*, the highest form of prayer, a wordless prayer in which we simply rest quietly in God's presence, basking in God's love. Intuition more than reasoning is involved here.

Informal Prayer

The easiest way to pray is to talk to God familiarly about whatever is on our minds, which is usually just the stuff of daily life. In the evening we can imagine God asking, "So, how was your day?" In heart-to-heart talks, we share with God our fears, desires, passions, dreams, disappointments, worries, joys, and sorrows. We are forthright with God, knowing that we will never shock him and that his love for us is unconditional. The Carmelite nun St. Thérèse of Lisieux admitted, "I say just what I want to say to God, quite simply, and he never fails to understand."

Making an Intention

Catholics believe in the communion of saints, that is, the saints in heaven, the souls in purgatory, and the faithful on earth bound together in the Body of Christ. One corollary of this belief is that the good performed by one member can be applied to another. In other words, we can "offer up" facets of our lives—our works, our prayers, our sacrifices, and our sufferings—for specific intentions and trust that God will apply them. For example, we can offer up a dreaded surgery for the intention of peace in the Middle East. This practice infuses meaning into our actions and in particular our sufferings. When we encounter a trial, we can always "kiss it up to God," that is, offer it to God and put it to good use.

EXTENDED PERIODS OF PRAYER

- An *octave* is eight days of prayer. Prayer for Christian Unity is an octave from January 18 through January 25 during which we pray that all Christians may be one. Christmas and the seven days following it constitute the Octave of Christmas.

- A *novena* is praying a certain prayer nine consecutive days or nine hours. Novenas began in imitation of the nine days that Mary and the disciples prayed while awaiting the coming of the Holy Spirit. People pray novenas to obtain a favor or to honor Jesus or a saint. A Christmas novena, for example, honors the nine months Jesus spent in Mary's womb.

- A *triduum* is three days of prayer that usually occurs before a special day. The three days before Easter (Holy Thursday, Good Friday, and Holy Saturday in Holy Week) are known as the Holy Triduum.

- A *retreat* is a period of prayer away from the busyness of life in which people concentrate on developing their relationship with God in silence and solitude. It is usually made under the guidance of a retreat director and can run from one to thirty days.

- A *day of recollection* is a short retreat that is usually centered around a theme. The retreat can last for one day or for part of the day.

Short and Long Prayers

One-line prayers called aspirations or ejaculations can be prayed throughout the day, lifting our minds and hearts to God in the midst of work. They are said to be like jewels added to our actions. Here are some of the most common aspirations:

Jesus!

Jesus, Mary, Joseph!

My Lord and my God!

Jesus, meek and humble of heart, make my heart like yours.

O sacrament most holy, O sacrament divine, all praise and all thanksgiving be every moment thine.

O Mary, conceived without sin, pray for us who have recourse to you.

My God and my all.

My Jesus, mercy.

Jesus, my God, I love you above all things.

Jesus, for you I live; Jesus, for you I die; Jesus, I am yours in life and in death.

Most Sacred Heart of Jesus, I place my trust in you.

O Heart of Jesus, burning with love for us, inflame our hearts with love for you.

Most Sacred Heart of Jesus, have mercy on us.

O Sacred Heart of Jesus I implore that I may ever love you more and more.

A ***litany*** is a rather long prayer invoking God or a saint under many titles. The invocations in each set are followed by the same response, such as "have mercy on us" or "pray for us." Popular litanies are the Litany of Loreto to the Blessed Virgin Mary, the Litany of the Sacred Heart, the Litany of the Holy Spirit, and the Litany of Saints.

4

Jesus,
Teacher of Prayer

As the Son of God, Jesus enjoyed an intimate relationship with his Father, and so naturally he had a vibrant prayer life. Jesus modeled prayer for us. He prayed the psalms both by himself and with others in the synagogue (Luke 4:16) and the Temple. But Jesus also prayed spontaneously, such as when he thanked his Father for his revelations (Matthew 11:25–26). Before undertaking his ministry, Jesus made a forty-day retreat in the desert. The Gospels also show Jesus praying before and during major events in his life:

- during his baptism (Luke 3:21–22),
- before choosing the twelve apostles (Luke 6:12–13),
- before the Transfiguration (Luke 9:28–31),
- before the raising of Lazarus (John 11:41–42),
- and in the garden before his passion and death (Mark 14:32–36).

Jesus prayed early in the morning while it was still dark

(Mark 1:35). Sometimes he even prayed all night (Luke 6:12), considered quite a feat by those of us who find one hour a challenge. Jesus prayed before meals (John 6:11, Luke 22:17–19). And he prayed for his friend Peter (Luke 22:31–32). At the Last Supper Jesus prayed for all of his disciples and all of us (John 17:1–26). Finally, Jesus prayed while he was hanging on the cross (Luke 23:34; Mark 15:34; Luke 23:46).

Besides being a model of prayer, Jesus taught several lessons on prayer:

- Jesus pointed out that we are not to pray in a showy, hypocritical way. Rather, we are to go to our room, close the door, and pray to our Father in secret.

- Jesus said that we are not to babble but to keep our prayers short and simple (Matthew 6:5–7).

- He taught us to ask and we will receive, seek and we will find, knock and the door will be opened (Matthew 7:7). In particular, he assured us that whatever we ask of the Father in his name we will receive (John 16:23), which is why so many of our prayers conclude with a phrase like "through Christ our Lord."

- Jesus also warned that not everyone who prays, "Lord, Lord," will enter heaven, but the ones who do his Father's will (Matthew 7:21).

- And, surprisingly, Jesus told us to pray for those who persecute us (Matthew 5:44), an act that either changes them or us.

Parable on Humble Prayer

In one parable that Jesus told (Luke 18:9–14) two men are praying in the Temple. One is a Pharisee, a protector of the Law. The other is a tax collector, whose profession was associated with theft and made him an outcast. The Pharisee boasts of his good deeds and gives thanks that he is not like sinners such as the tax collector. Meanwhile the tax collector beats his breast and can't even look up as he prays, "God, be merciful to me, a sinner." The tax collector's humble prayer is more pleasing to God.

Parables on Persevering Prayer

Two of Jesus' parables teach us to persevere in prayer. One of these (Luke 11:5–8) is about a man who has an unexpected visitor in the middle of the night and goes to his neighbor to beg bread so he can be hospitable. He pounds on the door until the neighbor relents and gives him bread. In the other parable (Luke 18:2–8) a widow who is being treated unjustly pleads with a judge to hear her case. Although the judge is a harsh man, he gives in to her just to stop her from hounding him.

THE OUR FATHER

When the apostles asked Jesus to teach them to pray, he gave us the Our Father, or the Lord's Prayer. This prayer has seven petitions. Three of them refer to God, and four to people. Here is an explanation of the words:

Our Father: We dare to address God as Jesus did, familiarly as our Father. Because the Father, Son, and Holy Spirit are one, we are addressing the whole Trinity. The "our" signifies our communion with all other believers.

Who art in heaven: Where God is, there is justice and perfect happiness. Heaven is our homeland and already exists in the hearts of the just.

Hallowed be thy name: "Hallowed" means holy or blessed. A person's name stands for the person himself or herself. In this statement we glorify God and ask that everyone live in a way that hallows God.

Thy kingdom come: God's kingdom or reign is one of peace, justice, and love. We pray that it will spread throughout the world. We pray for the final coming of Christ and the fullness of the kingdom.

Thy will be done: We pray that people will follow God's all-wise plan.

On earth as it is in heaven: In heaven angels and saints constantly do what is pleasing to God.

Give us this day our daily bread: Bread stands for what we need to live. We depend on the good God for all of our necessities. This bread can also signify the Eucharist.

And forgive us our trespasses: We ask God to forgive our sins and failings.

As we forgive those who trespass against us: A dangerous petition because we are asking God to forgive us to the extent that we forgive others.

And lead us not into temptation: We ask God to help us discern what is wrong and to keep us safe from whatever may lead us to sin.

But deliver us from evil: We petition God to protect us from evil, or the Evil One.

5

Setting the Stage
for Prayer

How carefully we plan the ambience for a special meal or a special event. We pay attention to decorations, sound, and scent to create just the right atmosphere. Certain conditions also contribute to a good prayer experience. The following are some to keep in mind.

Carving Out Time for Prayer

Nurturing our relationship with God through prayer is a challenge when our lives are hectic. But did you ever notice how we always find time to do the things we really want to do, such as work out or watch a certain television program? If we don't make an appointment with God for a specific prayer time, but relegate him to spare time, he's likely to get no time. Once we make a habit of praying at a certain time, if we ever skip it, we will miss it. Considering the weighty significance of prayer, it makes sense that we give it our first and best time.

Be Still and Know That I Am God
(Psalm 46:10)

Great things happen in silence. Flowers and babies grow, snow falls, and the sun rises. We need silence to calm down, to rest, and to think better. Likewise, we need quiet to pray and to hear God's soft voice. So when we pray, we turn off the cell phone, the television, and the radio, and silence the thoughts buzzing through our minds. We focus on God, whose name is Silence.

Alone with the Alone

Just as a married couple needs quality time alone together, sometimes we need to be alone with God for a close, intimate conversation. This means finding a place where other people won't distract us. We might drive to a quiet street and park or take a solitary walk in the woods. On a bus or in a crowded room we can be "alone" by closing our eyes.

Holy Place

It helps to have a special prayer place where we automatically fall into a mood for prayer. We might have a prayer corner in our house, or a chair that is our "prayer chair." The place where we meet God could be a certain room in the house, a place outside, a chapel, the library, a spot in the park, or a bench by the lake. This sanctuary can exist only in our mind! We can mentally construct a room designed in our favorite colors, furnished with our preferred kind of chair, and decorated with paintings and objects. This prayer room might feature a picture window with a spectacular view or a blazing fire in the fireplace. In our imagination we can enter that room, make ourselves comfortable, and then visualize Jesus joining us.

PRAYER AIDS

Any of the following objects will help keep us focused on prayer.

- A Bible, perhaps one with a beautiful cover, is God present in his Word.

- A crucifix reminds us of God's great love for us.

- A picture or statue of Jesus, Mary, or another saint is also helpful.

- A burning candle stands for the mystery of God or Christ as the light of the world.

- Incense (grains or a stick) symbolizes our prayers going to God as its smoke rises.

- Potpourri appeals to our sense of smell.

- A picture of a glorious nature scene or an item from nature such as flowers, a plant, seashells, rocks, or driftwood can make us think of God's presence.

These items can be placed on a lovely cloth. Some people like to hold a crucifix or other object as they pray. Music is also conducive to prayer.

Our Bodies at Prayer

Prayer is usually associated with kneeling, either on the floor or on a kneeler. This posture expresses humility before our great and awesome God. We can, however, pray in any of the following ways: standing, sitting up straight on a chair (not too comfortably), sitting cross-legged on the floor, walking, running, lying in bed, prostrate (face down on the floor), sitting on a prayer pillow, kneeling on a kneeler, sitting on our heels, or using a prayer stool (a small raised plank on which we sit with our legs under it).

Hands can be folded or resting open, palms up (in an attitude of reception) or palms down on our lap. We can extend our arms out to the side in the form of a cross. At times we might raise our arms to God, genuflect, or bow. The Lotus pose is another option: sitting with the legs crossed so that the feet rest at the bend of the knees, and then resting hands on heels with forefingers and thumbs touching to form a circle. On the other hand, we can dance before the Lord, imitating David who danced before the Ark of the Covenant. Involving our bodies in prayer is praising God with our whole being.

Calming Yourself for Prayer

Here are some ways to settle into prayer:

- Do something you find calming. You might walk slowly, listen to music, or crochet.

- Inhale slowly and deeply, count to five, and then exhale slowly. Repeat this three times.

- Relax your muscles. First tighten the muscles on the top of your head for a few seconds and then loosen them. Then do the same in turn for your forehead, eyes, mouth, cheeks, neck, shoulders, arms, hands, chest, thighs, lower legs, and feet.

- Imagine that you are floating on a cloud or down a river.

- Become aware of your mind. What is revealed to you?

- Mentally move from one part of your body to another, becoming conscious of the sensations in it.

- Be aware of the air as it passes through your nostrils.

- Listen to the sounds around you. Realize that God is sounding all around you.

- Hold an object. Use all your senses to become fully aware of it.

- Say your name over and over as if God is calling you.

Choosing a Name

Addressing God by a particular name at the beginning of prayer helps in focusing our attention and shaping our prayer. You might use Father, Gracious God, Spirit of God, Jesus, Savior, Creator, or come up with an original name for God.

Prayer Boosters

There are many kinds of prayer books on the market that can be a resource for prayer. Some are collections of prayers. Others offer a short meditation for each day based on the daily Scripture readings. Some Web sites also offer daily devotions, such as www.dailygospel.org and living-withchrist.us.

A Prayer List

Making a list of people and intentions that you want to pray for can help you remember them when you pray. You can keep the list in a prayer book or Bible where you will be likely to see it.

6

Times *to Pray*

Corrie Ten Boom asks, "Is prayer your steering wheel or your spare tire?" It's normal to pray during times of extreme emotion, such as when we are terrified, sad, or elated. Sometimes prayer comes unexpectedly in a flash, for example, when we behold a breathtaking sunset. Ideally prayer is a daily habit, carried out as regularly as we take three meals a day. Habits make it easier to do good things, but forming them takes time and persistence.

Specific Prayer Times

Most Catholics have a habit of praying at three main times:

In the morning. This might be our first and perhaps our best time to pray. We are rested, and the concerns of the day haven't yet occupied our minds or used up our hours, leaving none for prayer. In order to pray, some people set their alarm to rise a little earlier. And some even pray a little in bed before they begin to move. (See the Morning Offering on page 93.)

Before and after meals. We depend on God for the food that keeps us alive, so it's only courteous to be mindful of

A JESUIT EXAMINATION OF CONSCIENCE

The Jesuit way of making a nightly examination of conscience prompts us to make better moral choices during the day because we want to give ourselves a good report at night.

1. Recall God's presence and ask the Holy Spirit to enlighten you.

2. Think of things during that day that you are grateful for, and thank God. These can be small things like a beautiful rose in your garden and the joy of going to a concert or large things like a good report from the doctor.

3. Replay the day like a movie in your mind's eye, looking for times when you accepted God's grace and times when you didn't cooperate with it. Perhaps you can pat yourself on the back for letting someone take the parking spot you had your eye on or for biting your tongue when tempted to make a hurtful smart remark. On the other hand, maybe you recall with regret how in the checkout line when the person ahead of you was short of cash, you thought of offering to cover it, but then didn't.

4. Ask forgiveness for your failings.

5. Ask God for grace to respond better the next day. You could look ahead to situations you might face and decide on the best course of action.

God at mealtime. Before meals we ask God to bless our food, and after we've enjoyed our meals we thank him. These meal prayers are called "grace." It's always good to include in meal prayers an intercession for those who do not have enough to eat. (See the prayers before and after meals on page 93.)

In the evening before retiring. At night we thank God for the blessings of the day. We might do an examination of conscience, a review of our behavior that day, and then pray an act of contrition for any failings. To make an examination of conscience you might go through the ten commandments and consider whether you have been faithful in keeping each one. Or you might think of each place where you were that day and consider whether you were loving there: at home, at the office, in the store, at a party, at a game.

Sunday: A Day of Prayer

Sunday is our Sabbath, our day of rest. It is our day for worship—specifically for celebrating Eucharist—and for extra prayer. It's time to listen to God speak in creation, for example, by enjoying our backyard, by visiting a park or a zoo, or by using nature for recreation and going swimming, horseback riding, or skiing. Sunday is also the time to strengthen family and community ties and to do something for those in need. On Sunday we seek creative ways to say to God, "I love you too."

Other Occasions for Prayer

At certain times in life, such as those listed below, our hearts might naturally turn to God. Sometimes, though, at these times we might forget to tap into the power of prayer.

- facing a crisis

- making a serious decision

- on seeing a beautiful sight

- when we are tempted
- after having sinned
- when a friend or relative is sick or in trouble
- on receiving a special blessing
- before going on a journey
- when we're not getting along with someone

Filling Time

Odd moments can be used for prayer. During the day the many downtimes when we are forced to do nothing can turn into prayer moments. Here are some opportune times:

- on hold on the phone
- waiting for a red light to change
- standing in a checkout line
- waiting for a bus
- waiting for something to download
- in an elevator
- waiting for the doctor or dentist
- on the treadmill

Mechanical jobs like mowing the lawn and crocheting an afghan usually require little or no attention. Why not pray at the same time? In these cases, multitasking is good for your health. Some people like to pray on long, monotonous trips.

Pray Always

St. Paul exhorts us to "pray without ceasing" (1 Thessalonians 5:17). We can heed this advice throughout the day by being mindful of God, who is ever mindful of us. An analogy is a husband who is always aware of his beloved when she is working in another room, or even when he is miles away from her. He is with her in remembrance and feelings. Reminders—for example, a crucifix on the dashboard of our car or the name "Jesus" on a card beneath our computer screen—prompt us to think of God. One person has made touching a doorknob a cue to recall God's presence. God is never farther away than the inner recesses of our own hearts. As Meister Eckhart once noted, "God is at home. It is we who have gone out for a walk."

St. Teresa of Avila recommended that we imagine that the Risen Lord is by our side all during the day. We can communicate with him every so often, with or without words. Theophane the Recluse summed up this kind of prayer: "The hands at work; the mind and heart with God." Sometimes while engaged in something, we receive an impulse to pray. We should always try to cooperate with this actual grace as quickly as we answer our cell phones.

St. Paul advises, "Whether you eat or drink, or whatever you do, do everything for the glory of God" (1 Corinthians 10:31). When we offer ourselves and our lives to God—for example, by praying the Morning Offering—everything becomes a prayer. By making a conscious effort, our whole life can be prayerful.

Praying in the Home

The home is rightly called the domestic church. Prayer, therefore, should certainly be part of normal family life. Children learn to pray best by observing their parents pray and by praying with their parents. Some families schedule a time for weekly prayer together and take turns leading the prayers.

7

Challenges *to Prayer*

Some days it is easy to pray, and praying leaves us feeling upbeat and renewed. Then there are the other days when we are bored, restless, dry, or plagued by distractions. All we can muster is "Here I am, Lord." Hubert van Zeller commented that it helps to remember that "we go to pray not because we love prayer but because we love God." We can take comfort in these words: "Likewise the Spirit helps us in our weakness; for we do not know how to pray as we ought, but that very Spirit intercedes with sighs too deep for words" (Romans 8:26). One help to good prayer is realizing that Jesus is not just an idea or a hazy one-dimensional image, but a real, live person. The following are some common challenges that make it difficult to pray.

Misconceptions about Prayer

Some people are prayer-shy because they have the wrong impression of prayer. Here are some common misconceptions.

- *Prayer should be long.* **False!** Short prayers can be effective. What do people cry out when their house is on fire? They do not scream, "A conflagration is devastating my abode." They yell, "Fire!" Your most frequent prayer might be, "Help!" St. Augustine said, "A long speech is one thing, a long love another."

- *Prayer should result in a torrent of wonderful thoughts.* **False!** Perhaps the grace that comes from prayer is not an idea at all, but a moment of joy, a tear in the eye, a sense of peace, a desire, or a resolution.

- *Prayer should be formal.* **False!** St. Teresa of Avila advises, "Try not to let the prayer you make to such a Lord be mere politeness...avoid being bashful with God." Tevye in *Fiddler on the Roof* is a good example of informal prayer. To him prayer is not so much a duty but a visit with a friend. We don't have to try to impress God with grand words. He knows us through and through and loves us. By the way, being real and honest with God might mean giving full play to our emotions. This is how the psalmist prayed in the psalms of lament. For example, repeatedly in Psalm 13 he complained, "How long, O Lord? How long?"

- *Prayer is difficult.* **False!** James Finley recalls, "Merton once told me to quit trying so hard in prayer. He said, 'How does an apple ripen? It just sits in the sun.'" We needn't struggle to pray. Meister Eckhard says, "Get out of the way and let God be God in you." The Jesuit Thomas Greene describes the higher form of prayer as floating as opposed to swimming.

- *I am not worthy to speak to God.* **False!** Every person, though sinful, is a child of God, loved and redeemed by him. Jesus went out of his way to be with sinners.

- *Deep prayer is only for great saints.* **False!** All of us are called to be holy, to be saints. We are all redeemed and baptized. We do not have to be super intelligent or super good in order to experience, deep, profound prayer. God showers his gifts, including the gift of prayer, on whomever he wishes.

TRUE PRAYER

The test of true prayer is not how good it makes us feel, but whether we're doing God's will better. Prayer makes us more loving, more Christlike. The change in us may be subtle and slow, but it's there. In particular we will show the fruits of the Holy Spirit that St. Paul lists in Galatians 5:22: love, joy, peace, patience, kindness, generosity, faithfulness, gentleness, and self-control.

Bad Feelings

We don't always feel like praying. But it's precisely when we're discouraged, upset, or frustrated that we need to pray most and when we need God the most. Perhaps we resist praying because we think we "get nothing out of it." But remember, lovers are more intent on giving than on receiving. A passage from mystic Juliana of Norwich's *Revelation* encourages us to persevere through negative feelings:

> Our Lord is greatly cheered by our prayer. He looks for it, and he wants it….So he says, "Pray inwardly, even if you do not enjoy it. It does you good, though you feel nothing, see nothing, yes even though you think you are dry, empty, sick or weak. At such a time your prayer is most pleasing to me.

An antidote to dryness in prayer is to pray ready-made prayers. They might spark love in our hearts.

Distractions

Often when we pray, our minds flit from one distraction to another. We think about memories, fears, joyful experiences, or what we're going to have for dinner. The Buddhists refer to "the monkey mind," which darts from idea to idea like a monkey jumping from tree to tree. Sometimes our minds are fastened on one major concern. Maybe we finish praying the rosary and realize that we've spent the entire time thinking about a project we have to do. It often is a struggle to focus and refocus on prayer.

There's no need to feel guilty about distractions; they're part of human nature and keep us humble. When a novice was grieving about her distractions, St. Thérèse of Lisieux told her, "I, too, have many, but I accept all for love of the good God, even the most extravagant thoughts that come into my head." Not all distractions are bad. A distraction may be a grace in disguise, for example, if it's the solution to a problem or an idea for an act of charity you can perform. Sometimes distractions during prayer are like thoughts that enter our minds while we are conversing with friends. In both cases they do not disturb our conversations.

Sleeping

St. Thérèse of Lisieux explained that she did not regret sleeping during prayer. She pointed out that little children please their parents just as much when they sleep as when they are awake. The heavenly Father loves us as we sleep. Nevertheless, we might combat fatigue by eating a candy bar or drinking coffee.

STRATEGIES TO CONTROL DISTRACTIONS

- Pray at a quiet time and in a peaceful place. There will be fewer external distractions.

- At the outset, recall that you are in God's presence. Make yourself aware of God looking at you with love, and you will be more inclined to focus on him.

- Pray before a crucifix, a picture, or a lighted candle. The visual aid will keep your mind on prayer.

- Write a prayer. This demands concentration and therefore eliminates distractions.

- Pray out loud. This forces you to pay more attention to your words.

- If your distraction is important, jot it down so you can deal with it after prayer.

- Ignore the distractions as though they were clouds passing by. Focusing on them only makes them more irritating.

- Work your distraction into your prayer. For example, if you catch yourself thinking and worrying about your mom's upcoming surgery, begin interceding for her.

Restlessness

Even St. Teresa of Avila had trouble at prayer. She admitted shaking the hourglass during prayer to speed up the time. Sometimes we're tempted to cut our prayer time short, maybe because we're thinking of all the things we have to do. One man recounted that when he was tempted to end his prayer early, he forced himself to pray five minutes longer, and during those five minutes he had an extraordinary spiritual experience.

Busyness

Some days may be so jam-packed that we actually don't pray. A consoling thought then is that "the wish to pray is prayer itself" (George Bernanos).

God's Silence

Sometimes it seems that God doesn't hear our prayers. Then it's tempting to jump to these wrong conclusions: "There is no God," "I'm not a good pray-er," or even "God doesn't love me." Instead, consider that God has several ways of answering. Sometimes God says yes, but other times God says no. Sometimes God answers in a way that we don't expect—or recognize. God may say, "Not yet" or "I have a better idea." Also, as former president Jimmy Carter pointed out, God may say, "Are you kidding?"

It's possible that what we ask of God works counter to his grand plan of salvation—even though what we ask appears good to us. Then our request cannot be fulfilled. In this case it helps to realize that through any difficulties or sufferings God will be at our side.

Remember: When frustrated or discouraged with our prayer life, we can take heart: One thing we can pray for is the grace to pray well!

8

Liturgical *Prayer*

A noted theologian once declared that he could not have gotten through the challenges of recent years had it not been for his parish prayer group. Communal prayer is powerful. For one thing, Jesus promised, "Where two or three are gathered in my name, I am there among them" (Matthew 18:20). Moreover, witnessing others praying nurtures our own prayer. Another advantage of shared prayer is that bonds form among the group members so that they become a support for one another. The communal prayer par excellence is the Eucharist, where together as the people of God we praise and thank him. The Mass, all seven sacraments, and the Divine Office (also known as the Liturgy of the Hours), constitute the Catholic liturgy, or the public worship of the Church.

The Eucharist is our best and most perfect prayer, called the source and summit of Christian life. It is a mosaic of all forms of prayer: praise, thanksgiving, contrition, and intercession. The word *eucharist* means "thanksgiving." At Mass, we Catholics gather as the people of God to hear God's Word, to offer sacrifice, and to receive Jesus in Communion.

Our worship at Mass is accompanied by the worship of all the angels and saints and therefore shares in the liturgy of heaven.

Sacrifice and Meal

The Mass is of infinite value because it is an act of Jesus. On the night before he died, Jesus ate a special meal with his disciples. During it he took bread, blessed and broke it, and declared, "This is my body." He passed the sacred bread to his disciples. Then he took a cup of wine, blessed it, and said, "This is my blood of the new eternal covenant." He passed around the cup. Then Jesus commanded, "Do this in remembrance of me."

Ever since then, the followers of Jesus have been celebrating this memorial meal. We believe that, in doing so, the sacrificial death and resurrection of Jesus that saved the world are made present again. This time we are partners in our redemption. At Mass we are able to offer Jesus along with ourselves to the Father. Moreover, we believe that the bread and wine, through the power of the Holy Spirit and the actions of the priest, who represents Jesus, truly become the body and blood of Jesus. Therefore when we consume the sacred bread and wine in Communion, we are actually consuming Jesus. We become one with him and one with the other members of the Church who share the same food with us. This meal is a foretaste of heaven where, united with God forever, we will feast at the banquet of eternal life united with God.

Reading and reflecting on the Scripture readings of the Mass ahead of time is a good way to prepare for Mass. Serving the community in the Eucharist, for example as a lector or an extraordinary minister of Holy Communion, can also make the Mass more meaningful.

Holy Days of Obligation

Mass is so crucial to the health of the Church that Catholics are bound to celebrate it every Sunday, which is the Lord's Day, or at a Saturday vigil Mass. We also are obliged to participate in Mass on special feasts called holy days of obligation, which in the United States are these:

December 8: Immaculate Conception

December 25: Christmas

January 1: The Solemnity of Mary, Mother of God

Thursday of the Sixth Week of Easter: The Ascension (Celebrated on the following Sunday in most U.S. dioceses)

August 15: The Assumption

November 1: The Feast of All Saints

When January 1, August 15, or November 1 falls on a Saturday or a Monday, participation in Mass is optional.

Outline of the Mass

Introductory Rites

1. *Entrance procession:* The celebrant and other liturgical ministers process to the altar while the opening song is sung.

2. *Greeting:* All make the Sign of the Cross. Then priest greets us with a wish that God may be with us.

3. *Penitential rite:* We ask God to forgive our sins that separate us from him and others. Then we will be more ready to participate in Mass. We pray, "Lord, have mercy."

4. ***Glory to God*** (except during Advent and Lent): We praise God, beginning by repeating words of the angels on the first Christmas.

5. ***Opening prayer:*** We pray together silently. Then the priest prays aloud for the community.

Liturgy of the Word: The Table of the Word

1. ***First reading:*** This reading from the Old Testament is in harmony with the Gospel message.

2. ***Responsorial psalm:*** We respond to God's Word with a psalm.

3. ***Second reading:*** This New Testament reading is from an epistle or the Book of Revelation.

4. ***Alleluia:*** We stand and praise Jesus who is about to speak to us in the Gospel. This prayer is replaced with another acclamation during Lent.

5. ***Gospel:*** This main reading is from the Gospel according to Matthew, Mark, Luke, or John. In it we hear about the teachings and saving deeds of Jesus. When the Gospel is announced, we make a cross with our thumb over our forehead, lips, and heart.

6. ***Homily:*** The priest or deacon teaches us about the Scripture readings, relating Jesus' message to our lives.

7. ***Creed:*** We profess our faith.

8. ***General intercessions:*** In this prayer of the faithful we pray for the Church, civil authorities, the needy, the salvation of the world, and local needs.

Liturgy of the Eucharist: The Heart

1. ***Preparation of the gifts:*** Community members bring

up the gifts of bread and wine along with water and perhaps donations for the poor and for the Church. The priest prays over the gifts.

2. ***Eucharistic prayer:*** This prayer is the centerpiece of the Mass. The bread and wine become the body and blood of Jesus (the mystery called transubstantiation), and his sacrifice on the cross is re-presented.

   a. *Preface*—In our name the priest praises and thanks the Father for salvation or some aspect of it.

   b. *Holy, Holy*—With the angels we praise God.

   c. *Eucharistic prayer*—The priest asks God that the bread and wine may become Christ for the salvation of all who will receive him. He then repeats the words and actions of Jesus at the Last Supper (the consecration) as he offered the sacrifice of his body and blood. The priest recalls Christ's passion, death, and resurrection. The whole Church of heaven and Earth offers Jesus and themselves to the Father. We pray for all members, living and dead.

3. ***Communion Rite:*** We receive Jesus under the forms of bread and wine and become one with him and with all Church members.

   a. *The Lord's Prayer*—We pray for "our daily bread" (the Eucharist), for forgiveness of our sins, and for deliverance from evil.

   b. *The Sign of Peace*—We extend peace to those near us, usually by shaking hands and saying, "The peace of Christ be with you."

   c. *The breaking of the bread*—The sacred host is broken and the blessed bread and wine prepared to be shared with the community while the Lamb of God is prayed. The priest drops a piece of the sacred bread into the cup. Then he shows the sacred host to us, and we pray that we are not worthy to receive our Lord but can be healed by his words.

    d. *Communion*—The community processes up and shares in Jesus' body and blood.

    e. *Prayer after Communion*—The priest prays for the effects of the mystery just celebrated.

Concluding Rite

1. **Greeting and blessing:** The priest says, "The Lord be with you," and blesses us.

2. **Dismissal:** We are sent out to love and serve in the world. We thank God.

Church Etiquette

For Catholics a church is truly a house of God because we believe that Jesus is with us there in the sacred host reserved in the tabernacle. Near this Blessed Sacrament a candle (sanctuary lamp) burns constantly as a sign that God is present. Out of respect for God, it is customary to genuflect on the right knee and make the Sign of the Cross before entering and when leaving a pew. We also make this act of adoration when passing in front of the tabernacle. When a genuflection is not possible, a bow is made. In some parishes genuflecting is no longer practiced.

At the entrances of the church are holy water fonts. On entering and leaving the church, Catholics dip the fingers of their right hand in the holy water and make the Sign of the Cross with it. This is done in remembrance of baptism, when we became Christians and were cleansed of sin.

MASS LEXICON

Alb: long white robe the priest wears

Altar: table on which Mass is offered; it symbolizes Christ.

Altar cloth: large cloth that covers the altar

Ambo: lectern at which the readings are read

Antependium: decorated material that is hung in front of the altar

Book of the Gospels: book from which the Gospel is proclaimed at Mass; it is carried in procession.

Cassock: ankle-length robe worn by altar servers; priests wear it outside of Mass.

Chalice: cup for the wine

Chasuble: long, sleeveless vestment the priest wears over the alb; its color matches the season of the church year or the feast.

Ciborium: lidded cup that holds the hosts

Cincture: white rope that the priest ties around his waist over the alb

Corporal: linen about a foot square that has a red cross in the middle of the front; the Eucharist is placed on it on the altar.

Credence table: side table in the sanctuary for articles used at Mass, such as the bread and wine, cruets, and a bowl

Cruets: two small jars for the water and wine

Lavabo dish: deep plate for washing the priest's fingers

Lectionary: book of Scripture readings for Mass

Pall: linen-covered cardboard square that covers the chalice

Paten: plate, usually silver or gold, on which the hosts are placed

Processional cross: cross or crucifix that leads processions

Purificator: white cloth used to dry the priest's fingers and the vessels

Pyx: small, round container for a sacred host that is used to take Communion to the sick

Sacramentary: book of prayers and directives for the Mass

Sacristy: room where the vestments and vessels for Mass are stored

Sanctuary: area around the altar and tabernacle

Stole: long scarf the priest wears around his neck and over the chasuble; a deacon wears a stole over his left shoulder.

Surplice: white smock with wide sleeves worn by altar servers over a cassock; priests wear it for liturgical services other than the Eucharist.

Tabernacle: small closet that houses sacred hosts available for the sick, and for adoration by the faithful

In some churches you see candles burning in front of a statue or shrine. These are vigil lights, or votive candles, and are lit for a certain intention. We make a donation, light a candle, and pray. The flame symbolizes our prayers rising to God as long as the candle burns.

The Church Year

The celebrations of the Eucharist follow an annual cycle remembering the mystery of Jesus: the incarnation and his death and resurrection.

- The church year, or liturgical year, begins with the season of *Advent*, when we joyfully anticipate the comings of Jesus in history (at Bethlehem), in mystery (in the Eucharist and every day), and in majesty (at the end of time).

- During the *Christmas season* we celebrate the birth of Jesus. This season includes the Solemnity of Mary and the Epiphany.

- The days after the Christmas season are called *Ordinary Time* because the weeks are numbered with ordinal numbers, for example, the Third Sunday in Ordinary Time.

- In the spring the forty-day season of *Lent* begins with Ash Wednesday. This is a season of penance and preparation for commemorating the passion, death, and resurrection of Jesus. Lent culminates in Holy Week, which ends with the Holy Triduum days of Holy Thursday, Good Friday, and Holy Saturday.

- The fifty-day long *Easter season*, when we celebrate the resurrection of Jesus, begins with the Saturday Night Easter Vigil and concludes with the celebration of Pentecost, when we remember the descent of the Holy Spirit upon the Church.

- Another period of Ordinary Time follows.

Concomitant with these seasons is the **sanctoral cycle** of the church year during which we celebrate the feast days of the saints and other special feasts. The prayers of the Eucharist and the Divine Office follow this cycle.

The Divine Office

You may know that members of certain religious orders gather at midnight for prayer and that priests pray from a breviary. These people are praying the Divine Office, which is also known as the Liturgy of the Hours or Prayer of Christians. The Divine Office is the official daily prayer of the Church. These are the seven hours of the Office: Morning Prayer, Midmorning Prayer, Midday Prayer, Midafternoon Prayer, Evening Prayer, and Night Prayer. An additional Office of Readings can be prayed at any time. All Christians are invited to pray the Divine Office, at least Morning Prayer and Evening Prayer (formerly called Vespers). In some parishes people pray these prayers together. The Office is mainly readings from Scripture. It parallels the seasons and feasts of the liturgical year celebrated at our daily Masses. A booklet called an **Ordo** is a guide to the feasts and prayers for each day of the year. Because the hours of the Office are prayed all over the world around the clock, all time is sanctified.

9

Scriptural
Prayer

In the *Constitution on Divine Revelation* the Church states: "In the sacred books the Father who is in heaven comes lovingly to meet his children and talks with them" (21). If prayer is communing with God, what better way is there to enter into it than through God's Word? In the Bible God speaks directly to us in a personal way, revealing himself as a loving God. Reading Scripture, then, is listening to God and thereby coming to know and love him. We can use any verses as a launching pad to God by savoring the words and letting them penetrate our hearts. Furthermore, the Bible, especially the four Gospels, helps us to know Jesus. As St. Jerome said, "Ignorance of Scripture is ignorance of Christ." Reading the Bible puts us in touch with Jesus himself, who is called the Word of God. And, as someone observed, "A Bible that is falling apart usually belongs to someone who is not."

The *New American Bible* is the version used in Catholic liturgy. The *New Revised Standard Version*, however, is approved for both Catholics and Protestants and has more inclusive language.

Reading the Bible

When reading the Bible it helps to read the footnotes as well as commentaries, which are books that explain Scripture verses. Here are various ways to read the Bible:

- *Bit-by-bit* Read only one or two lines and sink into them.

- *Book-by-book* Read a book straight through.

- *Bird's eye* Read only the boldface headings in a book and then reflect on the impact of the whole.

- *One track* Read according to a theme such as prayer, faith, forgiveness, or justice. Use a concordance (a book of words in the Bible and where they occur) or another index to find references.

- *Methodical* Read the Bible from beginning to end.

- *Liturgical* Read the readings for the day's eucharistic celebration.

- *First Opening* (also called the lucky dip or Bible roulette) Open the Bible at random and read.

- *Father David Knight's method* Keep the Bible on your pillow and every night read just one verse. Some nights you might read more. Before you know it, you'll have read an entire book.

Prayers in Scripture

The Bible is a gold mine of ready-made prayers that we can adopt. There is Moses' prayer; Daniel's prayer; prayer of Jabez (1 Chronicles 4:10); the canticles of Zechariah, Mary, and Simeon in Luke's Gospel; the Lord's Prayer; lines like the words of the father asking for his son's healing: "I believe; help my unbelief," and prayers in the letters of Paul.

Of course, there is also the Book of Psalms, the prayer book of the Bible.

The Psalms

Dorothy Day, co-founder of the Catholic Worker movement claimed, "My strength returns to me with my morning cup of coffee and reading the psalms." These one hundred

WAYS TO PRAY THE PSALMS

- Pray the psalm aloud.
- Visualize each image in the psalm.
- After each line pause for a count of four.
- Pray a psalm from a Christian perspective: Jerusalem stands for the Church or for heaven, while the king is Jesus.
- Sing psalm-based hymns.
- Choose a psalm to fit your situation or emotion.
- When a psalm doesn't fit your situation, pray on behalf of someone whom it fits.
- For psalms that express hate and vengeance against enemies, pray about your spiritual enemies: your own sins, Satan, evils in the world, or sickness.
- Use the psalms as a springboard for conversation, as in this example:

  The Lord is my shepherd
  (How grateful I am that you kept me from falling on the ice the other day, Lord.)

  I shall not want.
  (Thank you for all your gifts, in particular these days a warm house. Please give me a heart that likes to share with others.)

and fifty prayers were originally sung, usually on the way to or in the Temple. Jesus and Mary, like all Jews, prayed them every day. Today quite a few favorite hymns are psalm verses in musical settings. There are so many song versions of the psalms not only because they are beautiful prayers but because we sing a responsorial psalm at every Mass. Psalms express all the feelings of our heart: praise, thanksgiving, contrition, lament, and love. Because the psalms are poetry, they are chock-full of colorful figurative language especially metaphors and similes. (For example, God is a mountain, he collects tears in a bottle, and enemies are like bees.) However, where our poetry has sound rhyme, the psalms have idea rhyme. A second line in a psalm may echo an idea from the first line in almost identical, opposite, or elaborating words.

Reflecting on Scripture

St. Teresa of Avila said, "We have such a great God that a single of his words contains thousands of secrets." To pray over just one verse of Scripture, consider the literal meaning of each main word, reflect on its meaning for you, and then speak to God about it. Here is an example of a reflection on one word:

"A lamp to my feet is your word" (Psalm 119:105)

Lamp…A lamp gives light and enables us to see so that we can carry on our normal activities when it is dark. A flick of the switch floods a room with light. Streetlights guide traffic in the dark; lights guide airplanes and ships. Thank you God for the gift of light and the light of your word. May you always be my light. May I walk in the light of your word, and may I be a light for others.

Memorizing Verses

Memorized Scripture verses will come to mind when they are needed. Use these techniques to "bank prayers":

- Reflect on the verse's meaning. Use a dictionary for unfamiliar words.
- Post a verse of the week on a refrigerator or mirror.
- Write the verse several times.
- Sing the verse to a tune.
- Make up motions to accompany the verse.
- If the verse is long, memorize one section at a time.
- Memorize right before you go to bed. The words will stay in your mind better.

10

More Prayer Styles

You might experiment with some of the following prayer styles that may be new to you.

Lectio Divina

Lectio divina is Latin for "sacred reading." In 2005, Pope Benedict XVI, speaking about lectio divina, stated, "If it is effectively promoted, this practice will bring to the Church—I am convinced of it—a new spiritual springtime." This prayer method flourished in Benedictine monasticism. However, it is not just for monks but for anyone. Lectio divina can be used not only with Scripture but also with spiritual books and articles, prayers, nature, and the experiences of our lives. Here are its four steps with their Latin names:

1. Lectio (reading) Receiving

Choose a passage from Scripture. Read slowly until an idea attracts you. The words will jump out at you.

2. Meditatio (meditating) Appropriating

Stop and mull over the idea that struck you. Repeat the words over and over, letting them sink into your heart and mind. Delve into the meaning of the words and savor them. Try to discover why those particular words attracted you. When the reason dawns on you, move into the next step.

3. Oratio (prayer) Responding

This step takes you from the head to the heart. Respond with a prayer according to how the words prompt you: a prayer of adoration, thanksgiving, sorrow for sin, petition, or love. Stay with these feelings. Let yourself desire God. Put yourself at the disposal of God's Spirit, preparing for God's action. Then you may return to the passage and continue reading, or you might be lifted into the next step.

4. Contemplatio (contemplation) Union

Be with God, enjoying his presence and letting him love you. Be alone with God in the great silence that is too deep for words. Here God takes over your faculties and assumes the lead. It may seem as though nothing is happening, but this is deceptive. Zen wisdom applies to this step: "Sitting still/ doing nothing, spring comes and the grass grows by itself."

The first three steps involve doing, while the last one is simply being. The first three are our actions; the last one is God's action. You may repeat steps several times or just do one step. When you are distracted or can't sustain the prayer, return to the passage and read it until another word strikes you. Guigo, a Carthusian, summarized the steps of lectio divina this way: "Seek in reading and you will find in meditation; knock in prayer, and it will be opened to you in contemplation." Blessed Dom Columba Marmion, O.S.B., summarized them like this: "We read under the eye of God until the heart is touched and leaps to flame."

Meditation

Catholic meditation is the direct opposite of the practices of meditation in vogue today. While modern methods aim to empty the mind, Catholic meditation fills the mind with thoughts of God, Scripture passages, or divine truths. It involves ruminating on these concepts like an animal chewing its cud. Rick Warren in *The Purpose Driven Life* says that if you know how to worry, you already know how to meditate. When meditating on a Scripture story, consider who, what, why, when, and how. This focused thinking stirs up our emotions and can lead to resolutions for a holier life. One spiritual writer advises that instead of thinking about God, it is better to think God. In other words, focus on God present to you personally and directly right now.

In his *Spiritual Exercises* St. Ignatius of Loyola taught the following form of meditation, which can be carried out using a Gospel event.

1. Ask for a particular grace.

2. Use your imagination and all five senses to fill in the details of the setting, see the characters and hear them speak, and watch the action. How do you feel toward Jesus in the scene? Replay the event in your mind as if you were participating. For instance, as you meditate on the Nativity, Mary might let you hold the newborn baby. When meditating on the washing of the feet at the last supper you might imagine that Jesus is kneeling to wash your feet.

3. Then discuss the event with God, the Father, the Son, the Holy Spirit, or Mary. This is called the colloquy.

4. Draw fruit from your reflection by applying the passage to your life and making a resolution.

Another way to meditate on a Gospel story is to imagine that you are one of the people in the story, experiencing what he or she is experiencing. For example, put yourself in the place of the woman who is caught in adultery, the blind beggar Bartimeus who is cured, Peter who is invited to walk on the Sea of Galilee, or a child on Jesus' lap.

USING IMAGINATION

There are different methods for using the imagination to facilitate prayer. In his journal Wordsworth recorded that when he was in a beautiful place, he often imagined Jesus next to him, for instance when he wrote his poem "Daffodils." Father George Maloney, SJ, takes people in an imaginary elevator down into the depths of their hearts. He slowly calls out the floors as they descend, then leaves them in silence to commune with God. Imagine Jesus with you in any of the following ways and then speak to him, even aloud, and imagine his reply.

- Sitting next to you
- Sitting on an empty chair in your room
- Meeting in a room mentally furnished to suit your taste
- Meeting at the seashore, in a garden, or on a mountaintop
- Sitting next to you in a boat
- Walking down a road with you
- Sitting with you in your favorite place

Teachers of prayer recommend taking away a morsel from our meditation, a word or phrase to nibble on during the day. This will make our prayer more fruitful and keep us more mindful of God.

Meditating on Art

Reflecting on a picture, such as a religious masterpiece or a nature scene, is a good way to pray. Icons, those stylized paintings cherished by the Eastern Churches, are called windows into heaven. They are created by artists who fast and pray. "The Trinity," "Christ the Pantocrator," and "Our Lady of Perpetual Help" are three well-known icons. When Fr. Henri Nouwen's couldn't pray, he sat for long hours before "The Trinity." He wrote, "I noticed how gradually my gaze became a prayer."

Praying Memories

Recall a time when you experienced God's love for you in a special way, when you felt close to God. Recall the place, the details of what happened, and how you felt. Then re-live that event in your imagination. Finally, speak to God about it.

We can put to rest painful or bothersome memories by reviewing them in the presence of God. Here is the process:

- Recall that God is present and rest in him.

- Think about how much God loves you.

- Ask the Holy Spirit to help you recall a past bad experience that negatively impacts your life today.

- Let the memory come to mind.

- Relive the event, this time as though Jesus is there

with you. In your imagination let Jesus act and talk to you during the experience.

- Thank Jesus for his love and healing.

Mantras: The Prayer of the Heart

A mantra is a short prayer—a word, phrase, or sentence—that is prayed repeatedly. Praying a mantra can free us from thinking so we can focus on God. When we are too tired, too weak, or too distressed to pray from a prayer book or to formulate our own prayers, we can pray a mantra. This simple way of praying has power to bring us relief and rest, to make us aware of God's consoling presence, and to open us to God. Its repetition is as soothing as the motion of a rocking chair, a swing, or waves on the shore. Praying mantras is like a child incessantly crying, "Mommy, I don't feel good," or a lover tirelessly repeating, "I love you." Gradually the mantras fall away leaving only the presence of God.

Mantras can be prayed silently, aloud, set to a melody, or synchronized with your breathing. Some people like to keep track of mantras with rosary beads. It is recommended that you sit relaxed with hands resting on your lap. Close your eyes and breathe deeply, letting all tension flow out of your body and mind. Focus on the Lord dwelling in you and then whisper the mantra slowly over and over, listening with love and desire. As you pray a verse, a word might change. For example, as you pray, "I love you, O Lord, my strength" (Psalm 18:1), all of a sudden you might realize that instead of praying "my strength" you are praying "my savior." Ponder the significance of the change.

Some mantras are reverse mantras, that is, rather than words we say to God, they are words that God is saying to us. For example, "Do not be afraid" (Matthew 28:5) is a comforting mantra before a stressful situation. Further examples are Isaiah 41:13, Isaiah 43:1, Matthew 28:20, John 11:25, John 16:33, and 2 Corinthians 12:9.

The Book of Psalms is a gold mine of mantras. However, they can be gleaned from other Bible books as well. See Isaiah 25:1, Isaiah 64: 8, Habakkuk 3:2, Luke 1:47, 1 Timothy 1:17, and John 6:68. Beautiful and meaningful mantras can also be lifted from the Mass prayers, others' prayers, favorite prayers, or hymns.

The Name Jesus

The simplest, most beautiful prayer is simply to say the name Jesus. This name contains the presence of the Son of God. It is "the name that is above every name" (Philippians 2:9). The Hebrew name Jesus means "Yahweh saves." By calling on Jesus by name, we bring him to us and within us. Repeating the name Jesus as a mantra is very powerful. Anthony de Mello, S.J., suggests saying Jesus as you inhale and saying a name of Jesus from Scripture or your own name for him as you exhale: Jesus, my rock; Jesus, my friend.

The Eastern Church gave us the Jesus prayer, which is repeated continuously and leads to union with God. It can be prayed inhaling on the first half and exhaling on the second half.

Lord Jesus Christ, Son of God,
  have mercy on me, a sinner.

Taizé Prayer

The monks of an ecumenical, international community in Taizé, France, have made chanted mantras popular. Their prayer sessions combine sung mantras, Scripture, and

silence. The Taizé community Web site gives this explanation of the short songs: "Using just a few words they express
a basic reality of faith, quickly grasped by the mind. As the
words are sung over many times, this reality gradually pen-
etrates the whole being. Meditative singing thus becomes
a way of listening to God." Recordings of Taizé songs are
available.

Centering Prayer

Centering prayer opens us to the gift of contemplation. It
is merely giving loving attention to God dwelling within us
and letting God do his work in us. Here are the steps:

1. Decide on a word or phrase that you will use to keep
   focused on God. You might choose Jesus, God, Abba,
   love, mercy, amen, listen, peace, my Lord and my God,
   or I love you. You will keep the same word throughout the prayer period.

2. Quiet down. Sit upright so your head is well supported
   by your spine. Be comfortable, but not so comfortable that you fall asleep. Keep your eyes gently closed
   so that energy is not wasted seeing. To relax, breathe
   slowly three times: exhale, take in fresh air, hold it,
   exhale.

3. Move toward God within you. Think only of God who
   is living deep within you and ponder God's love for
   you. Be present to God. Let his overwhelming love
   and goodness attract you. Rest in God's presence.

4. Respond with your chosen prayer word or phrase.
   Repeat this prayer word slowly in your mind.

5. Attend to God and enjoy God's presence. When you
   know you are aware of things other than God, or you

find yourself pestered by other thoughts, use your prayer word to gently bring you back. It functions like a tug on a kite string. Don't stop to think about how you're doing. Focus on giving God your loving attention.

6. When you are finished, pray a formula prayer like the Our Father or speak to God to ease the transition back to the world around you.

Journaling

A journal is a personal written record of thoughts, experiences, prayers, and blessings. It can be an aid to prayer or even an act of worship in itself. You don't have to be a good writer to keep a journal. A journal can

- be a way to meet our deeper selves, leading us to know and reflect on our beliefs and ideas, our needs and desires, the meaning of our lives,

- help in resolving conflicts and in working through a bewildering situation or feelings,

- heal wounds,

- be a place to examine the past and the present and thereby owning them more fully,

- change our self concept,

- and give us a chance to freely express ourselves.

To Keep a Journal

- Set aside time for it. When you don't have time to make an entry, jot down keywords on a special calendar.

- Write about the day's experiences and your reactions.

- Prime the pump by beginning with a starter question or open-ended statement.

- Let the ideas flow out of your mind and copy them. Don't try to control or edit them.

- Keep your journal private and be honest in what you write.

- Periodically reread your journal to see how God has spoken to you and has acted in your life.

Praying with Art

Some people use drawing, painting, or sculpting as a means of prayer. The creative action stirs and helps them express their thoughts and emotions. Even doodling can be a springboard to prayer. Doodle on paper and then look for a shape and pray about it.

Pilgrimages

Traveling to a sacred place is known as a pilgrimage. Pilgrimages were especially popular in the Middle Ages. Today people make pilgrimages to the Holy Land, where Jesus lived, to Rome, which is the heart of the Church today, or to a shrine such as Our Lady of Lourdes in France and Our Lady of Fatima in Portugal. You might make a pilgrimage to a shrine near you.

The Labyrinth

Not everyone could make a pilgrimage to Jerusalem in the Middle Ages, so labyrinths in cathedrals became a substitute. A labyrinth is one path that weaves around within a circle and ends at the center. People pray as they walk along the path to the center, which represents God. Then they

retrace their steps going back out to the world. The path represents the journey of life as it sometimes leads away from God and sometimes has us pass other people. The prayer along the way can vary. We can walk with a Scripture verse, a mantra, a feeling, a question, a petition, or simply walk, paying attention to our thoughts and feelings. The labyrinth can be walked slowly or even danced. Today some labyrinths are constructed outside. Some institutions have a canvas labyrinth that can be borrowed. There are labyrinths on cloth or paper that are "walked" with the finger as well as small metal labyrinths that are traced with a metal stick. Some Web sites contain labyrinths that can be walked using the mouse!

11

Catholic Devotions

Devotions are optional prayers and practices that people have developed over the centuries to express their faith. The *Catechism of the Catholic Church* encourages devotions because they help us grow in knowledge of the mystery of Christ and they enrich Christian life.

Devotions to Mary and the Saints

Catholics are known for honoring saints, people whom the Church has canonized, or officially declared as being in heaven. The saints are people who are proven to have lived a life of heroic virtue; some are martyrs, who have died for their faith. Of course, the queen of all saints is St. Mary, the Mother of God. The Church presents the saints to us to honor and especially to imitate. They are our models who inspire us to be holy too. We honor saints with feast days, make statues and paintings of them, wear medals of them, erect shrines to them, and name our children and churches for them. This honor takes nothing away from

God, for God is the creator of the saints and what is good in them is a reflection of God's goodness. In particular, the honor we give to Mary is pleasing to God, who filled her with grace and chose her to be his mother. We also ask the saints to intercede, or pray for us, just like we ask our friends and relatives on earth to pray for us. Because the saints are in heaven, they are closer to the ear of God! The Church has named saints as patrons, or caretakers of certain places, occupations, and situations. For example, the Immaculate Conception is the patroness of the United States, St. Martha is the patron of cooks, St. Anthony is a patron of lost things, and St. Jude and St. Rita are the patrons of impossible cases. The saint we are named for becomes our personal patron saint.

The Rosary

After September 11, 2001, Pope John Paul II urged everyone to pray the rosary "possibly every day, for peace, so that the world can be preserved from the wicked scourge of terrorism." He was echoing the words of Our Lady in her apparitions, most notably at Fatima, Portugal. The rosary is arguably the prayer most associated with Catholics outside of the Mass. We hang rosaries in our cars, and we are buried with the beads in our hands. A rosary's prayers are compared to a garland of roses offered to Mary—a token of our love. It is sometimes called a chaplet, which means "crown." The rosary is prayed especially during May, the month dedicated to Mary, and during October, the month of the rosary.

According to a legend, the rosary originated when Mary gave it to St. Dominic. Actually, Christians were praying on beads a hundred years before he lived. And the mysteries were formulated about two hundred years after his time. The Dominicans, however, were great promoters of the rosary.

HOW TO PRAY THE ROSARY

Make the Sign of the Cross with the crucifix, and if you wish, kiss the crucifix. On the crucifix pray the Apostles' Creed. Then on the single bead pray an Our Father. On the next three beads pray Hail Marys and pray a Glory Be at the end. Then for each decade, pray an Our Father on the single bead, pray ten Hail Marys, and end with a Glory Be.

An optional concluding prayer is the Hail, Holy Queen. (See page 88.)

Another option is to pray after each Glory Be the prayer that the Angel taught the three children at the apparitions of Fatima:

O my Jesus, have mercy on us, forgive us our sins, save us from the fires of hell. Take all souls to heaven, especially those most in need of thy mercy.

The rosary has evolved. Illiterate people who couldn't pray the hundred and fifty psalms in the Bible prayed 150 Our Fathers instead, keeping track of the prayers on strings of beads. When the Hail Mary prayer was composed, people began praying Hail Marys instead of Our Fathers. As they prayed, people meditated on events in the lives of Jesus and Mary, called mysteries, one mystery for each decade, or set of ten beads. There were three sets of mysteries: Joyful, Sorrowful, and Glorious. In 2002, Pope John Paul II gave us a fourth set called the Luminous Mysteries or Mysteries of Light, which cover the public life of Jesus. Most rosaries have five decades of beads. One-decade bracelets and rings are available too.

When we pray the rosary, we unite two forms of prayer: While our minds dwell on the mysteries, we say the formula prayers. The rhythmic praying is so peaceful that some people pray the rosary when they have trouble sleeping.

Because we meditate on the mysteries, the rosary is called the Gospel on beads. It's the custom to pray the mysteries as follows:

Monday, Saturday: Joyful Mysteries

Thursday: Luminous Mysteries

Tuesday, Friday: Sorrowful Mysteries

Sunday, Wednesday: Glorious Mysteries

We can also pray our own mysteries, such as the parable mysteries or the miracle mysteries, or mysteries that speak more to us and our lives.

To insure that we are *praying* and not merely saying the rosary, we might motivate ourselves by making an intention for the rosary. Or we might spend a minute before praying each decade concentrating on the mystery and asking for the grace to grow in a virtue related to it. Anther option is inserting a phrase after the word *Jesus* in each Hail Mary, relating the Hail Mary to the mystery being prayed. For example, for the Annunciation pray "...thy womb, Jesus, who was announced by an angel. Holy Mary..."

Joyful Mysteries

1. ***The Annunciation:*** The angel Gabriel was sent by God to announce to Mary that God had chosen her to be the Mother of Jesus the Savior, the Mother of God. (Luke 1:26–28)

2. ***The Visitation:*** Mary traveled to help her older relative Elizabeth who was pregnant with John the Baptist. When Elizabeth heard Mary's greeting, she cried out, "Blessed are you among women, and blessed is the fruit of your womb." Mary responded with the Magnificat. (Luke 1:39–45)

3. ***The Birth of Jesus:*** Mary gave birth to Jesus, wrapped him in swaddling clothes, and laid him in a manger. Angels appeared to shepherds and sang, "Glory to God in the highest heaven, and on earth peace among those whom he favors." (Luke 2:1–20)

4. ***The Presentation in the Temple:*** Mary and Joseph presented baby Jesus to God in the Temple as the law required. There, Simeon and Anna recognized that Jesus was the Savior. (Luke 2:22–38)

5. ***Finding of the Child Jesus in the Temple:*** As a twelve-year-old, Jesus remained in Jerusalem after Passover. On the way home they discovered he was missing. Three days later his parents found him in the Temple listening to teachers and asking them questions. (Luke 2:41–50)

The Luminous Mysteries

1. *The Baptism in the Jordan River:* Jesus had John the Baptist baptize him. John saw the heavens open and the Spirit of God descend on Jesus. A voice from heaven said, "This is my Son, the Beloved, with whom I am well pleased." (Matthew 3:17)

2. *The Wedding at Cana:* When wine ran out at a wedding, Mary appealed to Jesus and he worked his first miracle. He turned water into excellent wine. (John 2:1–12)

3. *The Proclamation of the Kingdom of God:* Jesus proclaimed the good news of God's love and salvation, saying "The time is fulfilled, and the kingdom of God has come near; repent, and believe in the good news." (Mark 1:15)

4. *The Transfiguration:* Jesus took Peter, James, and John up a mountain. While he prayed, his face changed and his clothing became dazzling white. He spoke with Moses and Elijah. (Luke 9:29)

5. *The Institution of the Eucharist:* On the night before he was crucified, Jesus shared a meal with his disciples and gave us the Eucharist. He offered himself for us under forms of bread and wine. In the Eucharist he remains with us. (Mark 14:22–26)

The Sorrowful Mysteries

1. *The Agony in the Garden:* After the Last Supper, Jesus went to a garden with Peter, James, and John. He prayed, "My Father, if it is possible, let this cup pass from me; yet, not what I want but what you want." He found the apostles sleeping. (Matthew 26:36–46)

2. *The Scourging at the Pillar:* Pontius Pilate, to satisfy the crowd, had Jesus scourged by the soldiers and then handed him over to be crucified. (Mark 15:6–16)

3. *The Crowning with Thorns:* Soldiers stripped Jesus and threw a scarlet cloak on him. They made a crown out of thorns and placed it on his head. They put a reed in his hand like a scepter. Kneeling before him, they mocked, "Hail, King of the Jews!" (Matthew 27:27–31)

4. *The Carrying of the Cross:* Jesus, weak from being whipped and beaten, could not carry his cross all the way to Calvary. Simon of Cyrene was forced to help him. (Mark 15:20–22)

5. *The Crucifixion:* At Golgotha Jesus was crucified between two criminals. He prayed, "Father, forgive them; for they do not know what they are doing." (Luke 23:33–46)

The Glorious Mysteries

1. *The Resurrection:* Early Sunday morning an angel appeared to two women at Jesus' tomb and said, "Do not be afraid; I know that you are looking for Jesus who was crucified. He is not here; for he has been raised, as he said." The angel sent the women to tell the disciples. (Matthew 28:1–10)

2. *The Ascension of Our Lord:* Jesus led his disciples to Bethany. He blessed them, then went apart from them and was taken up to heaven. (Luke 24:50–53)

3. *The Descent of the Holy Spirit:* When the disciples were gathered together on Pentecost, the Holy Spirit that Jesus had promised came to the Church with signs of fire and wind. The apostles boldly went out

and proclaimed the good news, and people of every language could understand them. (Acts 2:1–13)

4. *The Assumption of Our Lady into Heaven:* At the end of her earthly life, Mary was taken up body and soul into heavenly glory, as all faithful followers of Jesus will be someday.

5. *The Coronation of the Blessed Virgin Mary:* Mary, the holy Mother of God, reigns in heaven as Queen of All Saints. There she prays for and cares for the members of Christ.

A Scapular

Some people wear a cloth scapular or even several. Originally a scapular meant a part of the religious habit of some religious orders. It was a long piece of cloth that covered the front and back. Then the practice developed of wearing small scapulars as a sign of association with the spirituality of a particular religious order. These devotional scapulars are two small pieces of cloth connected by strings that are worn around the neck. Such scapulars are sacramentals and have indulgences attached to their use. A person is invested in a scapular by a priest. Of the seventeen known scapulars, the most widespread is the brown scapular of Our Lady of Mount Carmel, which usually bears her image. According to tradition, in 1251 Our Lady appeared to St. Simon Stock, a Carmelite, and promised that anyone (meaning the Carmelites) who wears this scapular until death will be saved. Wearing a scapular is not a superstitious practice that guarantees salvation no matter what the person does. Naturally the person who wears a scapular is already striving to live a good life. A scapular medal can substitute for a cloth scapular. The medal bears an image of the Sacred Heart on one side and Our Lady on the other.

The Stations of the Cross

You have probably noticed scenes of the crucifixion on the walls of your church or on posts in the parish yard. The Stations of the Cross, or Way of the Cross, is a popular devotion especially during Lent. Originally pilgrims walked the path of Jesus' passion and death in the Holy Land. This practice gained a plenary indulgence, which means that all punishment due for sin was cancelled. But not everyone could travel to Jerusalem. Therefore, the Church offered the same indulgence to someone who made the stations elsewhere. The stations can be prayed alone or with a group. In praying the fourteen stations, we trace Jesus' steps from his being condemned to death to his burial. Meditating on the supreme sacrifice Jesus made out of love for us moves our hearts to love and gratitude. The following are the traditional stations. Some people add a "fifteenth station" that refers to the resurrection.

First Station: Jesus Is Condemned to Death

Second Station: Jesus Carries his Cross

Third Station: Our Lord Falls the First Time

Fourth Station: Jesus Meets his Mother

Fifth Station: Simon of Cyrene Helps Jesus Carry his Cross

Sixth Station: Veronica Wipes the Face of Jesus

Seventh Station: Jesus Falls the Second Time

Eighth Station: Jesus Consoles the Women of Jerusalem

Ninth Station: Jesus Falls the Third Time

Tenth Station: Jesus Is Stripped of his Garments

Eleventh Station: Jesus Is Nailed to the Cross

Twelfth Station: Jesus Dies on the Cross

Thirteenth Station: Jesus Is Taken Down from the Cross

Fourteenth Station: Jesus Is Laid in the Tomb

We can pray our own prayers at each station or use a booklet. For public stations, usually one person carries the processional cross, flanked by persons carrying lighted candles. The leader and the three people process from station to station. The name of the station is stated, and we genuflect and pray, "We adore you, O Christ, and we bless you, because by your holy cross, you have redeemed the world." Then a reflection is made.

Eucharistic Devotions

Exposition, in which the sacred host is exposed in a holder called a monstrance, is a devotion from the thirteenth century. People come to gaze on the sacred host and adore Jesus present in this Blessed Sacrament. Some churches or chapels have perpetual adoration in which, day and night, people take turns praying before the exposed Blessed Sacrament. Making a "holy hour" has its roots in Jesus' question to the apostles during his agony in the garden when they fell asleep instead of praying with him: "Could you not stay awake with me one hour?" (Matthew 26:40) There is also Forty Hours Devotion, in which Jesus in the Blessed Sacrament is adored continually for three days. Exposition usually concludes with Benediction.

Benediction means "blessing." During the rite of Benediction people are blessed with the Blessed Sacrament.

For Benediction, first the priest places the sacred host in a monstrance and incenses it while a hymn of praise is sung. After a period of adoration, the priest again incenses the Blessed Sacrament and another hymn is sung. The priest then wraps his shoulders and hands in a humeral veil, lifts the monstrance, and silently makes the Sign of the Cross over the people with the sacred host. The service concludes with the Divine Praises, which are on page 97.

Visits to the Blessed Sacrament

A lovely Catholic custom is to drop into a church or chapel for a visit with Jesus in the Blessed Sacrament. Although unfortunately many churches now must be locked, there are still some open that enable us to strengthen our relationship with Christ and make an oasis for ourselves in the midst of a busy day.

The Sacred Heart of Jesus

Our heart pumps about 100,000 times a day to circulate our lifeblood, so it has come to symbolize the whole of a person. The heart is also a symbol of love. How fitting then that devotion developed to the Sacred Heart of Jesus. The heart of Jesus stands for Jesus himself as well as the total love of Jesus, divine and human. His heart was literally wounded for love of us when a soldier pierced it with a lance as Jesus hung on the cross.

In art the Sacred Heart appears as a wounded heart surrounded by thorns and surmounted by a cross and flames that signify Jesus' burning love for us. Rays emanating from the heart represent his divinity. The Sacred Heart may stand alone, or Jesus may be pointing to his Sacred Heart in his chest or holding his heart in his hand and gesturing toward it.

Devotion to the Sacred Heart became popular after St. Margaret Mary Alacoque, a Visitation nun in France, had visions of the Sacred Heart from 1673 to 1675. On the Feast of the Body and Blood of Christ, Jesus showed her his wounded heart and said, "Behold this heart burning with love for men." Although this devotion focuses on the love and mercy of Jesus, it also involves reparation for sin. In one of St. Margaret Mary's visions Jesus requested that a Communion of reparation be made on the first Friday of every month for nine consecutive months. He entrusted to her twelve promises to those who honor his Sacred Heart. The twelfth promise was salvation for those who make the first Fridays.

Wearing or carrying a Sacred Heart badge or wearing a Sacred Heart scapular shows devotion to the Sacred Heart. The Enthronement of the Sacred Heart, which is promoted by the Apostleship of Prayer organization, involves consecrating the family to the Sacred Heart. A statue of the Sacred Heart is placed in the home to remind the family members of their consecration.

The Immaculate Heart of Mary

Devotion to the Heart of Mary focuses on Mary as our model in faith, humility, and love of God. In 1830, Mary appeared to St. Catherine Labouré and asked to have a medal cast that is known as the Miraculous Medal. It bore her image on one side and on the other side the sacred hearts of Jesus and Mary.

First Saturdays

In her appearances at Fatima in 1917, Mary asked the children Lucy, Jacinta, and Francesco to promote the practice of going to Mass and receiving Communion as reparation for sin for five Saturdays in a row. This is the practice of the First Saturdays.

May Crownings

To honor Mary as queen of heaven and earth, a statue of her surrounded by spring flowers is crowned during a prayer service. This usually occurs in the month of May, which is Mary's month.

Divine Mercy

Devotion to Divine Mercy is centered on God's mercy and love for all, in particular, great sinners. People committed to this devotion trust in God's mercy, are grateful for it, and show mercy themselves. This devotion began with St. Faustina Kowalska (1905–1938), an uneducated nun in Poland. In February 1931, Faustina saw Jesus with one hand raised in blessing and the other touching his white garment at his heart. From that spot came forth two large rays, one red and one pale, which stood for the blood and water that streamed from his heart when it was pierced. Jesus directed Faustina to have an image made of him like this along with the words "Jesus, I trust in you." Jesus also requested that every day at 3 PM, the hour of his death, we remember his great mercy. In addition, Jesus asked Faustina that the Sunday after Easter be a feast dedicated to the Divine Mercy and promised graces to those who receive Communion on this day. He also asked that beginning on Good Friday a novena for this feast be made, and he gave an intention for each day of the novena. In the year 2000, Pope John Paul II declared the Second Sunday of Easter "Divine Mercy Sunday."

A chaplet is a string of prayer beads. Jesus asked St. Faustina to promote the praying of the Chaplet of Divine Mercy, which is prayed on a rosary as follows:

Pray the Our Father, the Hail Mary and the Apostles' Creed.

Then on the single bead before each decade pray
Eternal Father
I offer you the body and blood, soul and divinity
of your dearly beloved Son, Our Lord Jesus Christ,
in atonement for our sins and those of the whole world.

On the ten beads of each decade pray
For the sake of his sorrowful Passion,
have mercy on us and on the whole world.

Conclude by repeating three times
Holy God, Holy Mighty One, Holy Immortal One,
have mercy on us and on the whole world.

The Infant of Prague

The Infant of Prague devotion is centered on Christ's childhood and kingship. The statue depicts Jesus as a small child. He is crowned and holds a globe surmounted with a cross. His right hand is raised in blessing. The original statue, eighteen inches high, was brought from Spain and presented to Discalced Carmelite Fathers in Prague, Czechoslovakia, in 1628. During a war, the Fathers left and the statue was tossed with rubbish. When the Fathers returned, Fr. Cyril discovered it behind the altar. One day while praying by the statue Fr. Cyril heard Jesus say, "The more you honor me, the more I shall bless you." Today the statue stands in a gold and glass case at the Church of Our Lady of Victory in Prague. Carmelite sisters change its more than seventy outfits. Copies of the statue can be found in churches and homes today.

The Holy Child of Atocha

Devotion to the Santo Niño de Atocha is popular in Spain, Mexico, and the southwestern United States. He is usually seated and wears a wide-brimmed hat and a long ornate cloak. In one hand he holds a basket of roses or food and in the other a pilgrim's staff. This Holy Child helps prisoners, travelers, miners, the sick, and now immigrants. Legends surround the statue of the Santo Niño. When the town of Atocha in Spain fell to the Muslims, Christians were imprisoned. After the women prayed to Our Lady of Atocha, a child in pilgrim's clothing began bringing food to prisoners. People noticed that on the statue of Our Lady of Atocha, the shoes of the Child Jesus were worn and dusty. Whenever these shoes were replaced, they became soiled again.

MONTH DEDICATIONS

Traditionally Catholics have dedicated each month to a certain aspect of the faith as follows:

January: Holy Childhood

February: Holy Family

March: St. Joseph

April: Holy Spirit/Holy Eucharist

May: Mary

June: Sacred Heart

July: Precious Blood

August: Blessed Sacrament

September: Seven Sorrows of Mary

October: Holy rosary

November: Souls in purgatory

December: Immaculate Conception

Travelers told how a boy, dressed as a pilgrim, brought them food and supplies, traveled with them, and guided them to safe roads. Still another story recounts that an explosion in Fresnillo, Mexico, trapped many miners. When their wives went to church to pray, they saw that the child on the statue of Our Lady of Atocha was missing. When the miners emerged from the mine, they explained that a child had given them water and had showed them the way out. Later, there were other reports of a child helping miners. Each time the image of the child on Mary's lap was found to be dirty and his clothes torn.

Veneration of Relics

A relic is something related to a saint. It can be a part of a saint's body or something that has touched the saint. The relic is kept in a special container called a *reliquary* and is honored by the faithful.

Prayer for the Sick

The Anointing of the Sick is a sacrament through which Jesus continues his ministry of healing. Any Catholic who is seriously ill, elderly, or facing surgery may take advantage of the sacrament. It involves a blessing with the Oil of the Sick, the opportunity for the sacrament of Reconciliation, and Communion. The Communion given to a dying person is called *Viaticum*, a name that means "with you on the way."

Some parishes list the sick in the church bulletin and encourage everyone to pray for them. They might even involve the sick and the homebound in a ministry of prayer for the needs of the parish.

WEB SITES FOR PRAYER

The rosary www.theholyrosary.org

Stations of the Cross www.catholic.org

The Divine Office www.liturgyhours.org

The Spiritual Exercises
www.geocities.com/ourladyofthegraces

Sacred Space www.jesuit.ie/prayer

The Psalms www.praythepsalms.com

The labyrinth
www.the-peace-project.org/fingerlab.html, www.
yfc.co.uk/labyrinth/online.html, and www.grateful-
ness.org/labyrinth/index.htm

Prayers by saints www.catholicdoors.com

Sunday readings and short reflections
www.catholicnews.com/word2lif.htm

Retreat based on the Sacred Heart
www.sacredheartprayers.com

A prayer for each day of the year
prayingeachday.org

2,774 prayers www.catholicdoors.com/prayer

12

Catholic
Prayers

The Sign of the Cross

Catholics usually begin and end prayers with the Sign of the Cross. As we pray it, we trace a cross over ourselves with our right hand, touching our forehead, chest, left and right shoulders.

> *In the name of the Father,* (forehead)
> *and of the Son,* (chest)
> *and of the Holy* (left shoulder) *Spirit.* (right shoulder)
> *Amen.* (hands folded)

The Our Father

The early Christians prayed the Our Father, or the Lord's Prayer, three times a day. We pray it during Mass and the Liturgy of the Hours (Divine Office). The Lord's Prayer is also an excellent meal prayer. See page 19 for more information.

Our Father, who art in heaven, hallowed be thy name. Thy kingdom come, thy will be done on earth as it is in heaven. Give us this day our daily bread, and forgive us our trespasses as we forgive those who trespass against us. And lead us not into temptation, but deliver us from evil. Amen.

The Hail Mary

The first sentence of this prayer is Angel Gabriel's greeting to Mary at the Annunciation. The second sentence is Elizabeth's greeting to her at the Visitation. The Church added the names of Mary and Jesus. People added the rest of the prayer, which was approved by the Church in the sixteenth century.

Hail Mary, full of grace, the Lord is with you. Blessed are you among women and blessed is the fruit of your womb, Jesus. Holy Mary, Mother of God, pray for us sinners now and at the hour of our death. Amen.

Doxology

A doxology is a prayer of praise. The Great Doxology is the Gloria of the Mass. This is the shorter one:

Glory to the Father and to the Son and to the Holy Spirit. As it was in the beginning is now, and will be for ever. Amen.

Doxology *(traditional)*

Glory be to the Father and to the Son and to the Holy Spirit. As it was in the beginning, is now and ever shall be, world without end. Amen.

The Apostles' Creed

A creed is a statement of beliefs. The beliefs in the Apostles' Creed can be traced back to the apostles.

I believe in God, the Father almighty, creator of heaven and earth. I believe in Jesus Christ, his only Son, our Lord. He was conceived by the power of the Holy Spirit and born of the Virgin Mary. He suffered under Pontius Pilate, was crucified, died and was buried. He descended to the dead. On the third day he rose again. He ascended into heaven, and is seated at the right hand of the Father. He will come again to judge the living and the dead. I believe in the Holy Spirit, the holy catholic Church, the communion of saints, the forgiveness of sins, the resurrection of the body, and the life everlasting. Amen.

The Nicene Creed

This creed is usually the one prayed at Mass. It was composed at the Council of Nicea in 235 A.D. and revised at the Council of Constantinople in 381.

We believe in one God,
the Father, the Almighty,
maker of heaven and earth,
of all that is, seen and unseen.

We believe in one Lord, Jesus Christ,
the only Son of God,
eternally begotten of the Father,
God from God, Light from Light,
true God from true God,
begotten, not made,
one in Being with the Father.
Through him all things were made.

For us and for our salvation
he came down from heaven:
by the power of the Holy Spirit
he was born of the Virgin Mary,
and became man.

For our sake he was crucified under Pontius Pilate;
he suffered, died, and was buried.
On the third day he rose again
in fulfillment of the Scriptures;
he ascended into heaven
and is seated at the right hand of the Father.
He will come again in glory to judge the living and the dead,
and his kingdom will have no end.

We believe in the Holy Spirit, the Lord, the giver of life,
who proceeds from the Father and the Son.
With the Father and the Son he is worshiped and glorified.
He has spoken through the Prophets.
We believe in one holy catholic and apostolic Church.
We acknowledge one baptism for the forgiveness of sins.
We look for the resurrection of the dead,
and the life of the world to come. Amen.

Come, Holy Spirit

Invoking the Holy Spirit is recommended before reading the Bible or beginning a period of prayer. The Holy Spirit is our advocate and guide whose role is the sanctification of the Church.

Come, Holy Spirit, fill the hearts of your faithful
and enkindle in them the fire of your love.
Send forth your Spirit and they will be created
and you will renew the face of the earth.

O, God, who by the light of the Holy Spirit,

did instruct the hearts of the faithful,
grant that by the same Holy Spirit we may be truly wise
and ever enjoy his consolations.
Through Christ our Lord. Amen.

Acts of Faith, Hope, and Love

Faith, hope, and love are the three theological virtues that have to do with our relationship with God. In 1 Corinthians 13:1–13, St. Paul points out that the greatest of these is love.

Act of Faith

O my God, I firmly believe that you are one God in three divine Persons, Father, Son, and Holy Spirit; I believe that your divine Son became man and died for our sins, and that he will come to judge the living and the dead. I believe these and all the truths which the Holy Catholic Church teaches, because you revealed them, who can neither deceive nor be deceived.

Act of Hope

O my God, relying on your infinite goodness and promises, I hope to obtain pardon of my sins, the help of your grace, and life everlasting, through the merits of Jesus Christ, my Lord and Redeemer.

Act of Love

O my God, I love you above all things, with my whole heart and soul, because you are all good and worthy of all my love. I love my neighbor as myself for the love of you. I forgive all who have injured me and I ask pardon of all whom I have injured.

Acts of Contrition

The act of contrition is prayed during the sacrament of Penance and usually at night to express sorrow for the failings of that day. It's recommended to pray an act of contrition when in danger of death in order to set things straight with God before going to meet him face to face.

Act of Contrition

My God, I am sorry for my sins with all my heart. In choosing to do wrong and failing to do good, I have sinned against you whom I should love above all things. I firmly intend, with your help, to do penance, to sin no more, and to avoid whatever leads me to sin. Our Savior Jesus Christ suffered and died for us. In his name, my God, have mercy.

Act of Contrition (traditional)

O my God, I am heartily sorry for having offended you, and I detest all my sins because of your just punishments but most of all because they offend you, my God, who are all good and deserving of all my love. I firmly resolve, with the help of your grace, to sin no more and to avoid the near occasions of sin. Amen.

Act of Contrition (short form)

O my God, I am sorry for my sins because I have offended you whom I should love above all things. Help me to do penance, to do better, and to avoid anything that might lead me to sin. Amen.

For the Poor Souls

Catholics believe that our prayers can assist those who have passed from this life by shortening their stay in purgatory, a state of purification that makes one worthy of being in God's presence.

Eternal rest grant unto them, O Lord,
and let perpetual light shine upon them.
May they rest in peace. Amen.

Te Deum

This early Christian prayer is used on special occasions. The hymn "Holy God, We Praise Thy Name" is based on it.

You are God: we praise you;
You are the Lord: we acclaim you;
You are the eternal Father:
All creation worships you.
To you all angels, all the powers of heaven,
Cherubim and Seraphim, sing in endless praise:
Holy, holy, holy, Lord, God of power and might,
heaven and earth are full of your glory.
The glorious company of apostles praise you.
The noble fellowship of prophets praise you.
The white-robed army of martyrs praise you.
Throughout the world the holy Church acclaims you:
Father, of majesty unbounded,
your true and only Son, worthy of all worship,
and the Holy Spirit, advocate and guide.
You, Christ, are the king of glory,
the eternal Son of the Father.
When you became man to set us free
you did not spurn the Virgin's womb.
You overcame the sting of death,
and opened the kingdom of heaven to all believers.
You are seated at God's right hand in glory.
We believe that you will come, and be our judge.

Come then, Lord, and help your people,
bought with the price of your own blood,
and bring us with your saints
to glory everlasting.

Save your people, Lord, and bless your inheritance.
Govern and uphold them now and always.
Day by day we bless you.
We praise your name for ever.
Keep us today, Lord, from all sin.
Have mercy on us, Lord, have mercy.
Lord, show us your love and mercy;
for we put our trust in you.
In you, Lord, is our hope:
and we shall never hope in vain.

The Angelus

The Angelus, which takes its name from the Latin for the first words, is a reminder of the Annunciation of the Lord. Traditionally this prayer was recited three times daily—at 6 AM, noon, and 6 PM—while the "Angelus bell" was tolled.

V. *The Angel of the Lord declared unto Mary.*
R. *And she conceived of the Holy Spirit. (Hail Mary....)*

V. *Behold the handmaid of the Lord.*
R. *Be it done unto me according to thy word. (Hail Mary....)*

V. *And the Word was made Flesh.*
R. *And dwelt among us. (Hail Mary....)*

V. *Pray for us, O Holy Mother of God.*
R. *That we may be made worthy of the promises of Christ.*

Let us pray: *Pour forth, we beseech thee, O Lord, thy grace into our hearts; that, we to whom the incarnation of Christ,*

*thy Son, was made known by the message of an angel, may
by his passion and cross, be brought to the glory of his resurrection. Through the same Christ our Lord. Amen.*

Queen of Heaven (Regina Coeli)

The Regina Coeli, a Marian Easter prayer, replaces the
Angelus during the Easter season.

*Queen of heaven, rejoice, Alleluia.
For He whom thou didst deserve to bear, Alleluia.
Hath risen as He said, Alleluia.
Pray for us to God, Alleluia.*

V. *Rejoice and be glad, O Virgin Mary, Alleluia.*
R. *Because our Lord is truly risen, Alleluia.*

Let us pray: *O God, who by the resurrection of Thy Son,
Our Lord Jesus Christ, hast vouchsafed to make glad the whole
world, grant, we beseech Thee, that, through the intercession
of the Virgin Mary, His Mother, we may attain the joys of
eternal life. Through the same Christ Our Lord. Amen.*

Memorare

Memorare is Latin for "remember." This popular prayer to
Mary goes back to at least the fifteenth century.

*Remember, O most loving Virgin Mary, that never was it
known that anyone who fled to thy protection, implored thy
help, or sought thy intercession was left unaided. Inspired
with this confidence, I fly unto thee, O Virgins of virgins, my
Mother. To thee do I come, before thee I stand, sinful and sorrowful. O Mother of the Word Incarnate, do not despise my
petitions, but in thy mercy hear and answer me. Amen.*

Hail, Holy Queen (Salve Regina)

This Marian prayer probably originated in the tenth century.

> *Hail, Holy Queen, Mother of Mercy! Our life, our sweetness, and our hope! To thee do we cry, poor banished children of Eve; to thee do we send up our sighs, mourning and weeping in this valley of tears. Turn then, most gracious advocate, thine eyes of mercy toward us; and after this our exile show unto us the blessed fruit of thy womb, Jesus; O clement, O loving, O sweet Virgin Mary.*

Consecration to Mary

Through this prayer we entrust ourselves to Mary, knowing she will help us.

> *My Queen and my Mother, I give myself entirely to you; and to show my devotion to you, I consecrate to you this day my eyes, my ears, my mouth, my heart, my whole being without reserve. Wherefore, good Mother, as I am your own, keep me, guard me, as your property and possession. Amen.*

We Fly to Thy Patronage

This prayer is thought to be the oldest one to Mary.

> *We fly to thy patronage, O holy Mother of God. Despise not our petitions and our necessities, but deliver us from all dangers, O ever glorious and blessed Virgin.*

Magnificat

This is Mary's Canticle found in Luke 1:46–55. The Church prays it every day in Evening Prayer of the Divine Office.

> *My soul proclaims the greatness of the Lord,*

my spirit rejoices in God my Savior;
for he has looked with favor on his lowly servant.
From this day all generations shall call me blessed.
The Almighty has done great things for me,
and holy is his Name.
He has mercy on those who fear him in every generation.
He has shown the strength of His arm,
He has scattered the proud in their conceit.
He has cast down the mighty from their thrones,
and has lifted up the lowly.
He has filled the hungry with good things,
and the rich he has sent away empty.
He has come to the help of his servant Israel
for he has remembered his promise of mercy,
the promise he made to our fathers,
to Abraham and his children forever. Amen.

Litany of Loreto

This Marian prayer lists Mary's many titles. It is named for the shrine of Our Lady of Loreto in Italy, where it was prayed as early as 1558.

V. Lord, have mercy.
R. Lord, have mercy.

V. Christ, have mercy.
R. Christ, have mercy.

V. Lord, have mercy.
R. Lord, have mercy.

V. Jesus, hear us.
R. Jesus, graciously hear us.

V. God, the Father of Heaven,
R. have mercy on us.

V. God, the Son, Redeemer of the world,
R. have mercy on us.

V. God, the Holy Spirit,
R. have mercy on us.

V. Holy Trinity, One God,
R. have mercy on us.

Response: *pray for us.*

Holy Mary,
Holy Mother of God,
Holy Virgin of virgins,
Mother of Christ,
Mother of divine grace,
Mother most pure,
Mother most chaste,
Mother inviolate,
Mother undefiled,
Mother most amiable,
Mother most admirable,
Mother of good counsel,
Mother of our Creator,
Mother of our Savior,
Mother of the Church,
Virgin most prudent,
Virgin most venerable,
Virgin most renowned,
Virgin most powerful,
Virgin most merciful,
Virgin most faithful,
Mirror of justice,
Seat of wisdom,
Cause of our joy,

Spiritual vessel,
Vessel of honor,
Singular vessel of devotion,
Mystical rose,
Tower of David,
Tower of ivory,
House of gold,
Ark of the covenant,
Gate of heaven,
Morning star,
Heath of the sick,
Refuge of sinners,
Comforter of the afflicted,
Help of Christians,
Queen of angels,
Queen of patriarchs,
Queen of prophets,
Queen of apostles,
Queen of martyrs,
Queen of confessors,
Queen of virgins,
Queen of all saints,
Queen conceived without original sin,
Queen assumed into heaven,
Queen of the most holy rosary,
Queen of families,
Queen of peace,

V. *Lamb of God, who take away the sins of the world,*
R. *spare us, O Lord,*

V. *Lamb of God, who take away the sins of the world,*
R. *graciously hear us, O Lord.*

V. Lamb of God, who take away the sins of the world.
R. have mercy on us.

V. Pray for us, O holy Mother of God,
R. that we may be made worthy of the promises of Christ.

Let us pray. *Grant, we beg you, O Lord God, that we your servants may enjoy lasting health of mind and body, and by the glorious intercession of the Blessed Mary, ever Virgin, be delivered from present sorrow and enter into the joy of eternal happiness. Through Christ our Lord. Amen.*

Prayer to the Guardian Angel

Angels are pure spirits who worship God and do his bidding. Catholics believe that God has appointed an angel to care for each person. Jesus referred to these guardian angels (see Matthew 18:10).

Angel of God, my guardian dear,
to whom God's love commits me here,
ever this day be at my side,
to light and to guard, to rule and to guide. Amen.

Prayer to St. Michael

When Lucifer led some of the angels against God, St. Michael the Archangel successfully led the other angels in battle against them. He is the patron of the Catholic Church and is invoked especially in time of temptation.

Holy Michael, the Archangel, defend us in battle. Be our safeguard against the wickedness and snares of the devil. May God rebuke him, we humbly pray; and do you, O Prince of the heavenly host, by the power of God cast into hell Satan and all the evil spirits who wander through the world seeking the ruin of souls. Amen.

Morning Offering

Through the Morning Offering, we make our whole day an act of worship by offering it to God. The Holy Father suggests two intentions to pray for each month. These can be found at ewtn.com/faith/papalPrayer.htm.

O Jesus, through the immaculate heart of Mary, I offer you my prayers, works, joys and sufferings of this day in union with the holy sacrifice of the Mass throughout the world. I offer them for all the intentions of your sacred heart: the salvation of souls, reparation for sin, the reunion of all Christians. I offer them for the intentions of our bishops and of all the apostles of prayer, and in particular for those recommended by our Holy Father this month.

Prayer before Meals

Bless us, O Lord, and these thy gifts, which we are about to receive from thy bounty, through Christ, Our Lord. Amen.

Prayer after Meals

We give you thanks, almighty God, for all benefits. You live and reign now and forever. Amen.

Act of Spiritual Communion

At times when we are prevented from receiving Holy Communion, we can make the following act of spiritual communion to express our love for Jesus.

My Jesus, I believe that you are in the Blessed Sacrament. I love you above all things, and I long for you in my soul. Since I cannot now receive you sacramentally, come at least spiritually into my heart. As though you have already come,

*I embrace you and unite myself entirely to you; never permit
me to be separated from you.*

Canticle of Zechariah

Zechariah prayed this canticle when his son, John the
Baptist, received his name and was circumcised (Luke
1:68–79). The Church prays this prayer each day during
Morning Prayer of the Divine Office.

*Blessed be the Lord, the God of Israel;
he has come to his people and set them free.
He has raised up for us a mighty savior,
born of the house of his servant David.
Through his holy prophets he promised of old
that he would save us from our enemies,
from the hands of all who hate us.
He promised to show mercy to our fathers
and to remember his holy covenant.
This was the oath he swore to our father Abraham:
to set us free from the hands of our enemies,
free to worship him without fear,
holy and righteous in his sight all the days of our life.
You, my child, shall be called the prophet of the Most High,
for you will go before the Lord to prepare his way,
to give his people knowledge of salvation by the forgiveness of
    their sins.
In the tender compassion of our Lord
the dawn from on high will break upon us,
to shine on those who dwell in darkness and the shadow of
    death,
and to guide our feet into the way of peace.*

Prayer of Simeon (Benedictus)

Simeon prayed this prayer when he beheld the child Jesus who was being presented in the Temple (Luke 2:29–32). The Church prays this prayer each day in Night Prayer of the Divine Office.

Lord, now you let your servant go in peace.
Your word has been fulfilled.
My own eyes have seen the salvation
which you have prepared in the sight of every people,
a light to reveal you to the nations and the glory of your people
Israel. Amen.

Litany of the Holy Spirit

Lord, have mercy on us.
Christ, have mercy on us.
Lord, have mercy on us.
Father all powerful, have mercy on us.
Jesus, Eternal Son of the Father,
Redeemer of the world, save us.
Spirit of the Father and the Son, boundless life of both, sanctify
*   us.*
Holy Trinity, hear us.
Holy Spirit, who proceeds from the Father and the Son, enter
*   our hearts.*
Holy Spirit, who art equal to the Father and the Son, enter our
*   hearts.*

Response: *Have mercy on us.*

Promise of God the Father,
Ray of heavenly light,
Author of all good,
Source of heavenly water,

Consuming fire,
Ardent charity,
Spiritual unction,
Spirit of love and truth,
Spirit of wisdom and understanding,
Spirit of counsel and fortitude,
Spirit of knowledge and piety,
Spirit of fear of the Lord,
Spirit of grace and prayer,
Spirit of peace and meekness,
Spirit of modesty and innocence,
Holy Spirit, the comforter,
Holy Spirit, the sanctifier,
Holy Spirit, who governest the Church,
Gift of God, the most high,
Spirit who fillest the universe,
Spirit of the adoption of the children of God,
Holy Spirit, inspire us with the horror of sin,
Holy Spirit, come and renew the fire of the earth,
Holy Spirit, engrave thy law in our heart.
Holy Spirit, inflame us with the flame of thy love.
Holy Spirit, open to us the treasures of thy graces.
Holy Spirit, enlighten us with thy heavenly inspirations.
Holy Spirit, lead us in the way of salvation.
Holy Spirit, grant us the only necessary knowledge.
Holy Spirit, inspire in us the practice of good,
Holy Spirit, grant us the merits of all virtues.
Holy Spirit, make us persevere in justice.
Holy Spirit, be thou our everlasting reward.
Lamb of God, who takes away the sins of the world, pour
    down into our souls the gifts of the Holy Spirit.
Lamb of God, who takes away the sins of the world, grant us
    the spirit of wisdom and piety.

Come, Holy Spirit! Fill the hearts of thy faithful and enkindle in them the fire of thy love.

Let us pray. *Grant, O merciful Father that thy divine Spirit enlighten, inflame, and purify us, that he may penetrate us with his heavenly dew and make us faithful in good works; through Our Lord Jesus Christ, thy Son, who with thee in the unity of the same Spirit, lives and reigns forever and ever. Amen.*

The Divine Praises

The Divine Praises were originally composed in 1797 as a means of making reparation for profanity or blasphemy. Today this prayer is prayed at the conclusion of Benediction.

Blessed be God.
Blessed be His Holy Name.
Blessed be Jesus Christ, true God and true Man.
Blessed be the Name of Jesus.
Blessed be His Most Sacred Heart.
Blessed be Jesus in the Most Holy Sacrament of the Altar.
Blessed be the great Mother of God, Mary most Holy.
Blessed be her Holy and Immaculate Conception.
Blessed be her Glorious Assumption.
Blessed be the Name of Mary, Virgin and Mother.
Blessed be St. Joseph, her most chaste spouse.
Blessed be God in his Angels and in his Saints.

O-Antiphons

The O-Antiphons, which each begin with "O," address the Messiah using Old Testament titles and ask him to come. They are prayed on the last days before Christmas as the Alleluia verse of the Mass and in Evening Prayer. They form the verses of the Advent hymn "O Come, O Come Emmanuel."

December 16: *O Shepherd Who rules Israel, you Who led Joseph like a sheep, come to guide and comfort us.*

December 17: *O Wisdom that comes out of the mouth of the Most High, that reaches from one end to another, and orders all things mightily and sweetly, come to teach us the way of prudence!*

December 18: *O Adonai, and Ruler of the house of Israel, Who did appear to Moses in the burning bush, and gave him the law in Sinai, come to redeem us with an out-stretched arm!*

December 19: *O Root of Jesse, which stands for an ensign of the people, at Whom the kings shall shut their mouths, Whom the Gentiles shall seek, come to deliver us, do not tarry.*

December 20: *O Key of David, and Scepter of the house of Israel, that opens and no man shuts, and shuts and no man opens, come to liberate the prisoner from the prison, and them that sit in darkness, and in the shadow of death.*

December 21: *O Dayspring, Brightness of the everlasting light, Son of justice, come to give light to them that sit in darkness and in the shadow of death!*

December 22: *O King of the Gentiles, and desire thereof! O Cornerstone, that makes of two one, come to save man, whom You have made out of the dust of the earth!*

December 23: *O Emmanuel, our King and our Lawgiver, Longing of the Gentiles, and their salvation, come to save us, O Lord our God!*

December 24: *O You Who sit upon the cherubim, God of hosts, come, show Your face, and we shall be saved.*

Day by Day
(St. Richard of Chichester)

Thank you, Lord Jesus Christ,
For all the benefits and blessings you have given me,
For all the pains and insults you have borne for me.
Merciful Friend, Brother and Redeemer,
May I know you more clearly,
Love you more dearly,
And follow you more nearly,
Day by day.

Prayer for Peace
(attributed to St. Francis of Assisi)

Lord, make me an instrument of your peace.
Where there is hatred, let me sow love;
Where there is injury, pardon;
Where there is doubt, faith;
Where there is despair, hope;
Where there is darkness, light;
Where there is sadness, joy.

Divine Master, grant that I may not so much seek to be consoled, as to console; to be understood, as to understand; to be loved, as to love; for it is in giving that we receive, it is in pardoning that we are pardoned, it is in dying that we are born to eternal life.

Take, Lord, and Receive
(St. Ignatius Loyola)

Take, Lord, and receive all my liberty, my memory, my understanding, and my entire will. Whatever I have and possess you have given all to me. To you, Lord, I now return it. All is yours. Dispose of it according to your will. Give me only your love and your grace; I will be rich enough; that is enough for me.

To the Holy Spirit
(St. Augustine)

Breathe in me, O Holy Spirit,
that my thoughts may all be holy.
Act in me, O Holy Spirit,
that my work, too, may be holy.
Draw my heart, O Holy Spirit,
that I love but what is holy.
Strengthen me, O Holy Spirit,
to defend all that is holy.
Guard me, then, O Holy Spirit,
that I always may be holy. Amen.

Prayer before the Crucifix

Behold, O kind and most sweet Jesus, before your face I humbly kneel, and with the most fervent desire of soul, I pray and beseech you to impress upon my heart lively sentiments of faith, hope and charity, true contrition for my sins, and a firm purpose of amendment. With deep affection and grief of soul, I ponder within myself, mentally contemplating your five wounds, having before my eyes the words which David the Prophet spoke concerning you: "They have pierced my hands and my feet, they have numbered all my bones."

Soul of Christ (Anima Christi)

Soul of Christ, make me holy.
Body of Christ, save me.

Blood of Christ, fill me with love.
Water from Christ's side, wash me.
Passion of Christ, strengthen me.
Good Jesus, hear me.
Within your wounds, hide me.
Never let me be parted from you.
From the evil enemy, protect me.
At the hour of my death, call me.
And tell me to come to you
that with your saints I may praise you
through all eternity. Amen.

Prayer for Generosity
(St. Ignatius of Loyola)

Lord, teach me to be generous.
Teach me to serve you as you deserve;
to give and not to count the cost;
to fight and not to heed the wounds;
to toil and not to seek for rest;
to labor and not to ask for reward,
except to know that I am doing your will.

Radiating Christ
(John Henry Cardinal Newman)

Stay with me, and then I shall begin to shine as thou shinest;
so to be a light to others.
The light, O Jesus, will be all from you.
None of it will be mine.
No merit to me,
it will be you who shinest through me upon others.
O let me thus praise you, in the way which you love best,
by shining on all those around me.
Give light to them as well as to me;

light them with me,
through me.
Teach me to show forth your praise, your truth, your will.
Make me preach you without preaching—
not by words, but by example
and the fullness of the love which my heart bears to you.

Prayer of Trust
(Thomas Merton)

My Lord God, I have no idea where I am going.
I do not see the road ahead of me.
I cannot know for certain where it will end.
Nor do I really know myself,
and the fact that I think that I am following your will
does not mean that I am actually doing so.

But I believe that the desire to please you does in fact
please you.
And I hope I have that desire in all that I am doing.
I hope that I will never do anything apart from that desire.

And I know that if I do this,
you will lead me by the right road though I may know nothing
about it.

Therefore will I trust you always
though I may seem to be lost and in the shadow of death.
I will not fear, for you are ever with me,
and you will never leave me to face my perils alone.

St. Patrick's Breastplate (excerpt)

Christ be with me, Christ within me,
Christ behind me, Christ before me,
Christ beside me, Christ to win me;
Christ to comfort and restore me;

Christ beneath me, Christ above me,
Christ in quiet, Christ in danger,
Christ in hearts of all that love me,
Christ in mouth of friend and stranger.

Learning Christ

Teach me, my Lord, to be sweet and gentle
  in all the events of life,
  in disappointments,
  in the thoughtlessness of those I trusted,
  in the unfaithfulness of those on whom I relied.
Let me put myself aside,
  to think of the happiness of others,
  to hide my little pains and heartaches,
so that I may be the only one to suffer from them.
Teach me to profit by the suffering that comes across
  my path.
Let me so use it that it may make me patient, not irritable.
That it may make me broad in my forgiveness,
  not narrow, haughty and overbearing.

May no one be less good for having come within my influ-
ence. No one less pure, less true, less kind, less noble for
having been a fellow traveler in our journey toward eternal
life. As I go my rounds from one distraction to another, let me
whisper from time to time, a word of love to you. May my
life be lived in the supernatural, full of power for good, and
strong in its purpose of sanctity. Amen.

Serenity Prayer

God, grant me the courage to change the things I can change,
the serenity to accept those I cannot change,
and the wisdom to know the difference. Amen.

Prayer of St. Francis Xavier

O God, I love Thee for Thyself
 And not that I may heaven gain,
Nor yet that they who love Thee not
 Must suffer hell's eternal pain.
Thou, O my Jesus! Thou didst me
 Upon the Cross embrace.
For me didst bear the nails and spear
 And manifold disgrace;
And griefs and torments numberless
 And sweat of agony;
E'en death itself—and all for one
 Who was Thine enemy.
Then why, O blessed Jesus Christ,
 Should I not love Thee well:
Not for the sake of winning heaven,
 Or of escaping hell;
Not with the hope of gaining aught,
 Not seeking a reward,
But as Thyself hast loved me,
 O ever-loving Lord.
E'en so I love Thee, and will love
 And in Thy praise will sing
Solely because Thou art my God
 And my eternal King.

Mary Stuart's Prayer

Keep me, O God, from all pettiness;
let me be large in thought, in word, in deed.
Let me be done with fault-finding
and leave off all self-seeking.
May I put away all pretense
and meet others face to face

without self-pity and without prejudice.
May I never be hasty in judgment
and always generous.
Let me take time for all things,
and make me grow calm, serene, and gentle.
Teach me to put into action my better impulses,
straightforward and unafraid.
Grant that I may realize
that it is the little things of life that create differences,
that in the big things of life we are one.
And, O Lord God, let me not forget to be kind.

Prayer of Abandonment
(Charles de Foucauld)

My Father, I abandon myself to you.
   Do with me as you will.
Whatever you may do with me, I thank you.
I am prepared for anything, I accept everything.
Provided your will is fulfilled in me
   and in all creatures
I ask for nothing more, my God.
I place my soul in your hands.
I give it to you, my God,
with all the love of my heart
because I love you.
and for me it is a necessity of love,
this gift of myself,
this placing of myself in your hands
without reserve
in boundless confidence
because you are my Father.

Prayer to St. Joseph

O blessed Joseph, faithful guardian of my Redeemer, Jesus Christ, protector of your chaste spouse, the virgin Mother of God, I choose you this day to be my special patron and advocate and I firmly resolve to honor you all the days of my life. Therefore I humbly beseech you to receive me as your client, to instruct me in every doubt, to comfort me in every affliction, to obtain for me and for all the knowledge and love of the Heart of Jesus, and finally to defend and protect me at the hour of my death. Amen.

Catholic Prayer Words

adoration: our response of praise to God as we stand in awe of his great power, majesty, and goodness.

aspiration: a one-line prayer. Also called *ejaculation*.

Benediction: a Eucharistic devotion in which the Blessed Sacrament is exposed in a monstrance and we are blessed with it.

blessing: 1) a prayer calling on God to bestow gifts on a person or to ask God to mark a certain object or place, such as a house, with favor and divine protection; 2) can also set apart a place or object as a means of grace, for example rosaries are blessed; 3) can mean the act of God bestowing grace and favors, as when we say that God blesses us; 4) We can bless God, which means to praise God.

canticle: a sung prayer.

centering prayer: a silent prayer that focuses on God dwelling in the center of us. When attention wanders away from God, we use a word or phrase to come back to God. In essence, centering prayer is resting in God, enjoying God's presence. See *page 58*.

chaplet: a prayer form that uses beads, such as the rosary.

communal prayer: prayer that is prayed together.

contemplation: the highest form of prayer, a prayer without words. We are totally rapt in God's presence.

contrition: We express sorrow for sin, ask forgiveness, and intend to avoid sin in the future.

Divine Office: see *Prayer of Christians*.

Eucharistic devotions: special prayers in honor of the Blessed Sacrament, such as visits to the Blessed Sacrament and Benediction.

examination of conscience: a review of our life to notice where we have cooperated with God's grace and where we haven't. It is part of preparation for the sacrament of Reconciliation and recommended to be made each night.

exposition: making the sacred host visible for adoration by setting it in a monstrance.

grace before/after meals: In grace before meals we ask God to bless us and the food we are about to eat. In grace after meals we thank God for our food.

holy hour: an hour spent in prayer usually before the Blessed Sacrament.

indulgence: the canceling of the debt of satisfaction owed for sin by certain prayers or practices. It can be partial or plenary (complete).

intention: in prayer, it is some cause for which we offer intercessory prayer, such as world peace.

intercessory prayer: we ask for something on behalf of another person. Jesus is our intercessor because he constantly prays to the Father for us.

Jesus prayer: "Lord Jesus, Son of God, have mercy on me, a sinner." It is repeated over and over and can be synchronized with breathing.

journaling: writing one's thoughts and prayers, sometimes daily. This practice makes us more reflective and can produce a richer prayer life.

labyrinth: a circular path that leads to the center of a circle. As we walk the labyrinth, we pray on the way to the center, which stands for God, and on the way out into the world again. See *page 60.*

lectio divina: sacred reading, a method of prayer that leads to union with God in contemplation. The four steps are 1) read a passage and stop when a word or phrase catches your attention, 2) reflect on your "word," 3) respond to God in prayer, and 4) rest in the presence of God. See *page 51.*

litany: a long prayer invoking God, Mary or a saint under many titles.

liturgy: the public worship of the Church: the Eucharist, the sacraments, and the Divine Office.

Liturgy of the Hours: see *Prayer of Christians.*

mantra: a prayer word or phrase that is repeated continually.

May crowning: a Marian devotion in which a statue of Mary is crowned. This usually occurs in May because it is her month.

meditation: mental prayer in which we ponder God and the mysteries of our faith.

mental prayer: prayer that occurs silently in our minds as opposed to vocal prayer, which is said out loud.

novena: praying a prayer for nine consecutive days or nine hours. The practice is derived from the nine days that Mary and the disciples prayed waiting for the Holy Spirit to come at Pentecost.

O-antiphons: nine short prayers that invoke Christ using Old Testament titles. They are prayed in the liturgy on the days right before Christmas. See *page 97.*

octave: eight days of prayer.

petition: prayer asking God for something such as healing, a safe journey, or forgiveness. Jesus encouraged this kind of prayer.

pilgrimage: a journey to a holy place, such as the Holy Land or a shrine, for religious purposes.

prayer service: a celebration with a religious theme that incorporates Scripture, prayers, quiet time for reflection, and hymns.

procession: walking in honor of God usually within a liturgical or devotional service. For example, there are processions within the Mass, and on Good Friday people may process outside with a cross or statue of Christ.

Prayer of Christians: also called the Liturgy of the Hours and the Divine Office, the official daily prayer of the Church in which the entire day is sanctified. Priests and some religious are obliged to pray it, and all Christians are invited to pray it. There are seven times or hours when these prayers are prayed.

psalms: the 150 prayer-songs in the Bible's Book of Psalms. They are the Jewish prayer book, and have been adopted by

Christians. The psalms, which are Hebrew poetry, express the whole gamut of stances we have toward God: praise, lament, contrition, and thanksgiving.

Raccolta: a book that is collection of indulgenced Catholic prayers and practices. It was last published in Rome in 1898.

retreat: a period of time when we withdraw from everyday life and activities to focus on God and our relationship with God. A retreat can be a half day or as long as thirty days. Usually it has various prayer activities, including time for quiet prayer, talks by a retreat director, the celebration of the Eucharist, and the sacrament of Penance.

rosary: a Marian prayer in which we meditate on mysteries in the life of Christ while praying Our Fathers, Hail Marys, and Glory Bes on a circle of beads. Mary asked us to pray the rosary in her appearances at Lourdes and Fatima.

sacramental: a blessing or an object that has been blessed and whose use brings graces through the merits of Jesus and the prayers of the Church.

scapular: an indulgenced sacramental, two small pieces of cloth connected by strings that are worn around the neck. It shows devotion, usually to Our Lady, and is worn continually. After a person has been invested in a cloth scapular by a priest, a scapular medal may be substituted for it.

Stations of the Cross: Way of the Cross, a devotion in which we remember Jesus' passion as we walk from station to station and pray. Each of the fourteen stations has a cross and art depicting one event of the passion.

spiritual bouquet: a gift of prayers and good works. It usually lists the numbers of prayer and good works that are being offered for the recipient.

spontaneous prayer: informal prayer, vocal prayer that is not written down, prayed by rote using a formula prayer, or rehearsed.

Taizé prayer: the Taizé method of praying originated with an ecumenical community of monks in Taizé, France. It mainly consists of chanting short prayers over and over alternating with periods of quiet prayer.

thanksgiving: a main purpose of prayer. We express our gratitude to God for all his loving acts of creation and redemption.

triduum: three days of prayer, such as the Holy Week Triduum of Holy Thursday, Good Friday, and Holy Saturday/Easter Sunday.

veneration of a relic: relics are parts of a saint's body, something a saint has used, or material that has been touched to a saint. These are displayed in a case called a reliquary and people may venerate them in a ritual of prayer.

Viaticum: the Communion that a dying person receives

vigil light: votive candle, a candle that is lit for an intention. A prayer is said and a donation is made. The flame represents the prayer rising to heaven.

vocal prayer: prayer prayed aloud.